Preface

Welcome to the CTET Paper 2 Class VI to VIII Child Development and Pedagogy Book!

Teaching is a journey of learning, discovery, and personal growth. This book is designed to support you on that journey as you prepare for the Central Teacher Eligibility Test (CTET). Whether you are an aspiring educator or looking to enhance your knowledge, this book will equip you with essential concepts, strategies, and insights to excel in the exam and in your future teaching career.

Our goal is to make your learning experience meaningful and effective. Each chapter in this book has been carefully crafted to engage both your curiosity and critical thinking, covering core topics essential for the CTET exam. Along the way, you will find opportunities to reflect on best practices in education, the role of teachers in shaping society, and the importance of fostering an inclusive and supportive learning environment.

Table of Contents

Chapter 1: Questions

1. **Which of the following best describes child development?**

a) Physical growth only

b) A continuous process of change and growth

c) Development that stops after adolescence

d) A set of unrelated changes

Answer: b) A continuous process of change and growth

2.**What is the relationship between development and learning?**

a) Learning influences development, and development affects learning

b) Development occurs only after learning stops

c) They are independent processes

d) Learning is unrelated to development

Answer: a) Learning influences development, and development affects learning

3. **Which principle explains that development occurs from the head to the feet?**

a) Cephalocaudal principle

b) Proximodistal principle

c) Maturation principle

d) Sequential development principle

Answer: a) Cephalocaudal principle

4. **Which type of development focuses on thinking, memory, and reasoning?**

a) Physical development

b) Social development

c) Cognitive development

d) Emotional development

Answer: c) Cognitive development

5. **Which principle of development states that children grow at their own pace?**

a) Development is uniform for all

b) Development follows a set timeline

c) Development is individualized

d) Development stops at a certain age

Answer: c) Development is individualized

6. **Which principle of development explains that development proceeds from simple to complex?**

a) Development is static

b) Development follows sequential patterns

c) Development is unpredictable

d) Development stops in adulthood

Answer: b) Development follows sequential patterns

7. **Which area of development involves learning to form relationships with others?**

a) Physical development

b) Cognitive development

c) Social development

d) Maturation

Answer: c) Social development

8. **According to the proximodistal principle, development occurs:**

a) From the head downward

b) From the center of the body outward

c) Only in the limbs

d) From bottom to top

Answer: b) From the center of the body outward

9. **Which principle of development states that children develop skills in stages?**
a) Development is uniform across all children
b) Development is stage-based
c) Development follows a flexible timeline
d) Development stops with age
Answer: b) Development is stage-based

10. **Which principle states that development occurs throughout life?**
a) Development stops in adulthood
b) Development ends in adolescence
c) Development is lifelong
d) Development is complete at birth
Answer: c) Development is lifelong

11. **Which of the following is an example of a hereditary factor?**
a) Height
b) Quality of education
c) Friendships
d) Nutrition
Answer: a) Height

12. **Which environmental factor can influence development?**
a) Eye color
b) Family income
c) DNA structure
d) Blood type
Answer: b) Family income

13. **Which of the following best describes the role of heredity in child development?**
a) It determines all abilities and behavior
b) It provides genetic potential for development
c) It only influences emotional development
d) It is unrelated to development
Answer: b) It provides genetic potential for development

14. **How does environment affect development?**
a) It only affects physical development
b) It influences all areas of development, including social and emotional growth
c) It has no impact on learning
d) It only affects the child's friends
Answer: b) It influences all areas of development, including social and emotional growth

15. **Which of the following illustrates the interaction of heredity and environment?**
a) Genetic disorders that cannot be altered
b) A child's height influenced by both genes and nutrition
c) Learning abilities determined only by parents' genes
d) Emotional behavior that never changes
Answer: b) A child's height influenced by both genes and nutrition

16. **Which agent plays the primary role in early childhood socialization?**
a) School
b) Family
c) Media
d) Peer groups
Answer: b) Family

17. **What does the process of socialization help children learn?**
a) Scientific theories
b) Social norms and values
c) Mathematics formulas
d) Motor skills only
Answer: b) Social norms and values

18. **Peers play an important role in socialization by:**
a) Providing access to education
b) Teaching complex subjects
c) Offering opportunities to develop social skills
d) Replacing family influence
Answer: c) Offering opportunities to develop social skills

19. **What is the result of successful socialization?**
a) Children become isolated from society
b) Children learn to conform to societal norms
c) Children become independent from all relationships
d) Children avoid social interactions
Answer: b) Children learn to conform to societal norms

20. **Which of the following is an example of primary socialization?**
a) Learning to solve math problems in school
b) Developing table manners at home
c) Watching a movie with friends
d) Attending a professional workshop
Answer: b) Developing table manners at home

21. **Which cognitive ability develops during Piaget's sensorimotor stage?**
a) Abstract thinking
b) Object permanence

c) Moral reasoning
d) Problem-solving skills
Answer: b) Object permanence

22. **Which stage in Kohlberg's moral development focuses on societal rules?**
a) Pre-conventional stage
b) Conventional stage
c) Post-conventional stage
d) Egocentric stage
Answer: b) Conventional stage

23. **Vygotsky's concept of the Zone of Proximal Development (ZPD) refers to:**
a) Skills a child can perform independently
b) Skills a child can achieve with guidance
c) Skills beyond a child's capability
d) Tasks unrelated to learning
Answer: b) Skills a child can achieve with guidance

24. **According to Piaget, children in the preoperational stage:**
a) Can think logically about abstract concepts
b) Are limited by egocentrism
c) Develop advanced mathematical skills
d) Understand complex cause-and-effect relationships
Answer: b) Are limited by egocentrism

25. **What is the key idea in Vygotsky's theory?**
a) Development happens in isolation
b) Learning is a social process
c) Cognitive development is fixed by age
d) Intelligence cannot be developed
Answer: b) Learning is a social process

26. **What is the focus of child-centered education?**
a) Teacher-led lectures
b) Developing learning based on children's interests and abilities
c) Memorization and repetition
d) Assigning the same task to all students
Answer: b) Developing learning based on children's interests and abilities

27. **Progressive education emphasizes:**
a) Standardized testing only
b) Hands-on learning and critical thinking
c) Passive listening to lectures
d) Teacher dominance in the classroom
Answer: b) Hands-on learning and critical thinking

28. **Which of the following is a principle of child-centered education?**
a) Focus only on academic achievement
b) Children should actively participate in their own learning
c) Teachers must avoid student interactions
d) Assigning the same homework to all learners
Answer: b) Children should actively participate in their own learning

29. **In progressive education, learning is viewed as:**
a) Memorizing facts for exams
b) A continuous and experiential process
c) Limited to textbooks only
d) Teacher-led with no student input
Answer: b) A continuous and experiential process

30. **Which method aligns with progressive education?**
a) Inquiry-based learning
b) Rote memorization
c) Multiple-choice testing only
d) Lecture-based instruction
Answer: a) Inquiry-based learning

31. **Which theory of intelligence was proposed by Howard Gardner?**
a) Theory of General Intelligence
b) Theory of Multiple Intelligences
c) Emotional Intelligence Theory
d) Cognitive Load Theory
Answer: b) Theory of Multiple Intelligences

32. **Which of the following is NOT one of Gardner's multiple intelligences?**
a) Logical-Mathematical Intelligence
b) Spatial Intelligence
c) Genetic Intelligence
d) Musical Intelligence
Answer: c) Genetic Intelligence

33. **What does emotional intelligence refer to?**
a) Memorizing facts under pressure
b) Understanding and managing emotions effectively
c) Intelligence related to physical activities
d) Intelligence for academic success only
Answer: b) Understanding and managing emotions effectively

34. **What is the critical perspective of traditional IQ tests?**
a) They measure all forms of intelligence accurately
b) They overlook important aspects like creativity and emotions

c) They assess only motor skills
d) They predict future success perfectly
Answer: b) They overlook important aspects like creativity and emotions

35. **Which intelligence type relates to self-awareness and understanding one's emotions?**
a) Logical-Mathematical Intelligence
b) Interpersonal Intelligence
c) Intrapersonal Intelligence
d) Naturalistic Intelligence
Answer: c) Intrapersonal Intelligence

36. **According to Vygotsky, what is the role of language in thought development?**
a) Language is irrelevant to thought processes
b) Language and thought are interdependent
c) Thought develops first, followed by language
d) Language only affects memory
Answer: b) Language and thought are interdependent

37. **What is meant by cognitive flexibility?**
a) The ability to learn only one way
b) The capacity to switch between different concepts or ideas
c) The ability to follow strict rules
d) Ignoring alternative viewpoints
Answer: b) The capacity to switch between different concepts or ideas

38. **How can teachers encourage meaningful language development in children?**
a) By focusing only on grammar rules
b) By providing opportunities for dialogue and discussion
c) By avoiding conversations with students
d) By assigning repetitive writing tasks
Answer: b) By providing opportunities for dialogue and discussion

39. **Which theory explains that language influences how people perceive the world?**
a) Social Learning Theory
b) Linguistic Relativity Hypothesis
c) Constructivism
d) Behaviorism
Answer: b) Linguistic Relativity Hypothesis

40. **Which area of the brain is primarily involved in language production?**
a) Hippocampus
b) Amygdala
c) Broca's Area
d) Cerebellum
Answer: c) Broca's Area

41. **What does it mean to say that gender is a social construct?**
a) Gender roles are biologically determined
b) Society creates roles and expectations for each gender
c) Gender identity never changes
d) Genetics determine all behavior
Answer: b) Society creates roles and expectations for each gender

42. **Which of the following reflects individual differences among learners?**
a) All children learn at the same rate
b) Each student has unique abilities, interests, and learning styles
c) Learning is identical for all students
d) Intelligence levels are the same for everyone
Answer: b) Each student has unique abilities, interests, and learning styles

43. **What is the significance of understanding individual differences in education?**
a) To assign the same work to all students
b) To develop strategies that address each learner's needs
c) To eliminate differentiated instruction
d) To ensure that all students score the same
Answer: b) To develop strategies that address each learner's needs

44. **Which of the following is an example of gender bias in the classroom?**
a) Encouraging all students to participate equally
b) Assuming boys are better at math than girls
c) Providing equal opportunities for both genders
d) Assigning tasks based on students' interests
Answer: b) Assuming boys are better at math than girls

45. **How can teachers address individual differences effectively?**
a) By using the same teaching strategy for all students
b) By differentiating instruction based on student needs
c) By focusing only on high achievers
d) By avoiding flexible teaching methods
Answer: b) By differentiating instruction based on student needs

46. **What is the purpose of formative assessment?**
a) To provide feedback for improving student learning
b) To assign final grades only
c) To compare students with each other
d) To conduct national-level exams
Answer: a) To provide feedback for improving student learning

47. **What is the goal of school-based assessment?**
a) To focus on national-level competitions
b) To assess students continuously throughout the year

c) To eliminate classroom assessments
d) To focus only on theoretical knowledge
Answer: b) To assess students continuously throughout the year

48. **Which of the following is a tool used in school-based assessments?**
a) Standardized national exams
b) Portfolios
c) Only multiple-choice quizzes
d) University entrance exams
Answer: b) Portfolios

49. **Which type of assessment is conducted at the end of a learning period?**
a) Diagnostic assessment
b) Formative assessment
c) Summative assessment
d) Peer assessment
Answer: c) Summative assessment

50. **What does 'assessment for learning' focus on?**
a) Providing feedback to enhance the learning process
b) Evaluating students at the end of the course
c) Comparing students' grades
d) Giving only standardized test scores
Answer: a) Providing feedback to enhance the learning process

51. **What is the purpose of formative assessment?**
a) To assign final grades
b) To monitor and improve student learning continuously
c) To compare students' performance across schools
d) To conduct national exams
Answer: b) To monitor and improve student learning continuously

52. **Which type of assessment provides feedback to students during the learning process?**
a) Summative assessment
b) Diagnostic assessment
c) Formative assessment
d) Aptitude test
Answer: c) Formative assessment

53. **What is the goal of summative assessment?**
a) To provide feedback during learning
b) To measure students' overall learning at the end of a unit
c) To diagnose learning difficulties
d) To offer continuous feedback
Answer: b) To measure students' overall learning at the end of a unit

54. **Which assessment method involves students evaluating their peers?**
a) Teacher evaluation
b) Peer assessment
c) Summative assessment
d) Diagnostic assessment
Answer: b) Peer assessment

55. **What does diagnostic assessment help teachers identify?**
a) Strengths and weaknesses in students' prior knowledge
b) Students' preferences for group work
c) Whether students enjoy the subject
d) Students' behavior patterns
Answer: a) Strengths and weaknesses in students' prior knowledge

56. **What is an essential feature of school-based assessment?**
a) Focus on final exams only
b) Continuous evaluation throughout the academic year
c) Only written assessments
d) National-level standardized testing
Answer: b) Continuous evaluation throughout the academic year

57. **Which tool is commonly used in formative assessment?**
a) End-of-term exams
b) Observation checklists
c) College entrance tests
d) National aptitude exams
Answer: b) Observation checklists

58. **What is the key purpose of self-assessment?**
a) To compare scores with peers
b) To help students reflect on their learning progress
c) To determine final grades
d) To eliminate teacher feedback
Answer: b) To help students reflect on their learning progress

59. **Which of the following is an example of a summative assessment?**
a) End-of-semester exam
b) Weekly journal entries
c) In-class discussion feedback
d) Self-reflection activities
Answer: a) End-of-semester exam

60. **Which assessment type focuses on understanding students' initial abilities?**
a) Diagnostic assessment
b) Summative assessment

c) Peer assessment
d) Portfolio assessment
Answer: a) Diagnostic assessment

61. **What is the role of a teacher in child-centered education?**
a) To dictate every aspect of learning
b) To act as a facilitator guiding students' learning
c) To focus only on standardized tests
d) To prevent student-led discussions
Answer: b) To act as a facilitator guiding students' learning

62. **Which learning strategy emphasizes student participation and collaboration?**
a) Group projects and discussions
b) Rote memorization
c) Passive listening to lectures
d) Standardized testing
Answer: a) Group projects and discussions

63. **What is the main focus of child-centered learning?**
a) Teacher-centered instruction
b) Developing students' abilities and interests
c) Memorization of textbooks
d) Achieving uniform scores
Answer: b) Developing students' abilities and interests

64. **Which teaching strategy aligns with inquiry-based learning?**
a) Assigning open-ended projects and experiments
b) Focusing on multiple-choice questions
c) Providing direct answers to students
d) Assigning repetitive tasks
Answer: a) Assigning open-ended projects and experiments

65. **How do children benefit from problem-based learning?**
a) They memorize content more effectively
b) They develop critical thinking and real-world problem-solving skills
c) They avoid working in teams
d) They become dependent on teacher guidance
Answer: b) They develop critical thinking and real-world problem-solving skills

66. **What is the goal of inclusive education?**
a) To teach all students using identical methods
b) To integrate students of all abilities into mainstream classrooms
c) To separate students with disabilities
d) To focus only on academic performance
Answer: b) To integrate students of all abilities into mainstream classrooms

67. **Which approach is practical for teaching students with learning difficulties?**
a) Ignoring their challenges
b) Differentiated instruction tailored to individual needs
c) Assigning the same task to all students
d) Giving only verbal lectures
Answer: b) Differentiated instruction tailored to individual needs

68. **What is an Individualized Education Plan (IEP)?**
a) A plan designed to meet the unique needs of a specific student
b) A curriculum followed by all students
c) A behaviour management system
d) A list of school rules
Answer: a) A plan designed to meet the unique needs of a specific student

69. **How can teachers promote inclusion in the classroom?**
a) By assigning additional tasks to struggling students
b) By encouraging collaboration among students of all abilities
c) By focusing only on high achievers
d) By limiting group work
Answer: b) By encouraging collaboration among students of all abilities

70. **Which strategy is effective for addressing the needs of gifted learners?**
a) Providing additional challenges and enrichment activities
b) Reducing their workload
c) Ignoring their progress
d) Assigning only routine tasks
Answer: a) Providing additional challenges and enrichment activities

71. **What is intrinsic motivation?**
a) Motivation driven by external rewards
b) Motivation that comes from within, driven by personal satisfaction
c) Motivation based on peer approval
d) Motivation triggered by punishment
Answer: b) Motivation that comes from within, driven by personal satisfaction

72. **What type of motivation is triggered by rewards and recognition?**
a) Intrinsic motivation
b) Extrinsic motivation
c) Internal motivation
d) Reflective motivation
Answer: b) Extrinsic motivation

73. **How can teachers foster intrinsic motivation in students?**
a) By offering only external rewards
b) By creating meaningful and engaging learning experiences

c) By comparing students' grades
d) By using punishment as a motivator
Answer: b) By creating meaningful and engaging learning experiences

74. **What role does curiosity play in learning?**
a) It hinders student progress
b) It promotes deeper exploration and understanding
c) It discourages independent thinking
d) It is irrelevant to the learning process
Answer: b) It promotes deeper exploration and understanding

75. **How can teachers support students who fear failure?**
a) By assigning less challenging tasks
b) By encouraging effort and celebrating small successes
c) By avoiding feedback entirely
d) By focusing only on perfect outcomes
Answer: b) By encouraging effort and celebrating small successes

76. **What is the primary focus of child-centred education?**
a) Emphasizing memorization of facts
b) Encouraging active participation and individual interests
c) Following a rigid curriculum without flexibility
d) Focusing only on teacher-led instruction
Answer: b) Encouraging active participation and individual interests

77. **What is the role of the teacher in a progressive classroom?**
a) To act as a facilitator, guiding students' learning
b) To give direct answers without student input
c) To rely only on lectures and textbooks
d) To evaluate students through exams only
Answer: a) To act as a facilitator, guiding students' learning

78. **Which strategy is commonly used in child-centred learning?**
a) Rote memorisation
b) Project-based learning and inquiry-based activities
c) Solely focusing on final exams
d) Assigning the same task to all students
Answer: b) Project-based learning and inquiry-based activities

79. **Which approach aligns with child-centred education?**
a) Teacher control of every learning decision
b) Allowing students to explore their questions and ideas
c) Relying exclusively on standardised tests
d) Limiting student involvement in planning
Answer: b) Allowing students to explore their questions and ideas

80. **Which educational theory supports the idea of learning through hands-on activities?**
a) Behaviorism
b) Constructivism
c) Psychoanalysis
d) Cognitive dissonance
Answer: b) Constructivism

81. **According to Gardner, which intelligence involves sensitivity to words and language?**
a) Musical intelligence
b) Linguistic intelligence
c) Interpersonal intelligence
d) Logical-mathematical intelligence
Answer: b) Linguistic intelligence

82. **Which of the following is an example of bodily-kinesthetic intelligence?**
a) Writing poems
b) Solving math problems
c) Performing dance routines
d) Identifying emotions
Answer: c) Performing dance routines

83. **What is the critical principle of Gardner's theory of multiple intelligences?**
a) Intelligence is a single, fixed ability
b) Intelligence consists of multiple independent abilities
c) Intelligence is solely determined by genetics
d) All individuals possess the same type of intelligence
Answer: b) Intelligence consists of multiple independent abilities

84.**How can teachers address individual differences among students?**
a) By assigning the same tasks to all students
b) By differentiating instruction based on student needs
c) By focusing only on high-performing students
d) By limiting creative tasks in the classroom
Answer: b) By differentiating instruction based on student needs

85. **What does interpersonal intelligence involve?**
a) Understanding one's own emotions
b) Understanding and interacting effectively with others
c) Solving complex math problems
d) Developing physical coordination
Answer: b) Understanding and interacting effectively with others

86. **What is a significant goal of formative assessment?**
a) To assign final grades
b) To provide feedback that improves learning

c) To replace all standardised exams
d) To measure a student's behaviour only
Answer: b) To provide feedback that improves learning

87. **What is the primary feature of Continuous and Comprehensive Evaluation (CCE)?**
a) Focus only on end-of-year exams
b) Assess students regularly in both academic and non-academic areas
c) Use only written assessments
d) Ignore student behaviour and social skills
Answer: b) Assess students regularly in both academic and non-academic areas

88. **Which type of assessment provides feedback during the learning process?**
a) Summative assessment
b) Diagnostic assessment
c) Formative assessment
d) Peer evaluation
Answer: c) Formative assessment

89. **What is the critical purpose of summative assessment?**
a) To monitor students' progress during a unit
b) To evaluate students' learning at the end of a course or term
c) To eliminate the need for feedback
d) To focus only on classroom participation
Answer: b) To evaluate students' learning at the end of a course or term

90. **Which tool is commonly used in school-based assessment?**
a) National-level exams
b) Portfolios and project work
c) Competitive exams
d) Standardized aptitude tests
Answer: b) Portfolios and project work

91. **What is the primary goal of inclusive education?**
a) To exclude students with learning challenges from mainstream education
b) To ensure that all students, regardless of abilities, are included in the learning process
c) To focus only on academic achievers
d) To reduce the number of students in classrooms
Answer: b) To ensure that all students, regardless of abilities, are included in the learning process

92. **How can teachers support students with learning difficulties?**
a) By ignoring their individual needs
b) By providing targeted interventions and personalised support
c) By assigning only oral tasks
d) By excluding them from group activities
Answer: b) By providing targeted interventions and personalised support

93. **What is an effective strategy for teaching students with special needs?**
a) Giving the same assignments as others without modifications
b) Using differentiated instruction to meet their unique needs
c) Assigning fewer tasks to reduce expectations
d) Limiting social interaction in the classroom
Answer: b) Using differentiated instruction to meet their unique needs

94. **Which of the following best describes an Individualized Education Plan (IEP)?**
a) A general plan for all students
b) A personalised plan to meet the specific needs of a student
c) A list of classroom rules
d) A behaviour management tool
Answer: b) A personalised plan to meet the specific needs of a student

95. **Which teaching strategy promotes inclusion?**
a) Group activities that allow students of all abilities to participate
b) Assigning tasks only to high achievers
c) Separating students based on abilities
d) Ignoring diverse learning needs
Answer: a) Group activities that allow students of all abilities to participate

96. **According to Piaget, children in the preoperational stage are limited by:**
a) Abstract thinking
b) Egocentrism
c) Logical reasoning
d) Symbolic thought
Answer: b) Egocentrism

97. **Which type of learning occurs through observation and imitation?**
a) Behaviorist learning
b) Social learning
c) Cognitive learning
d) Discovery learning
Answer: b) Social learning

98. **What is an essential element of problem-based learning?**
a) Pre-defined answers
b) Real-world problems that encourage critical thinking
c) Memorizing solutions from textbooks
d) Avoiding group discussions
Answer: b) Real-world problems that encourage critical thinking

99. **How can teachers encourage students to become problem solvers?**
a) By always giving them answers
b) By encouraging exploration and inquiry

c) By limiting access to challenging tasks
d) By focusing only on exams
Answer: b) By encouraging exploration and inquiry

100. **Which learning approach focuses on solving real-world problems?**

a) Project-based learning

b) Rote learning

c) Lecture-based teaching

d) Test-oriented learning

Answer: a) Project-based learning

Chapter 2: Questions

101. **Which is an example of collaborative learning?**

a) Students working in groups to complete a task

b) Students taking individual quizzes without discussion

c) Students copying notes from the board

d) A teacher delivering a lecture with no student interaction

Answer: a) Students working in groups to complete a task

102. **How can teachers promote creativity in the classroom?**

a) By encouraging open-ended tasks and projects

b) By limiting students to multiple-choice tests

c) By discouraging group work

d) By focusing only on standardised tests

Answer: a) By encouraging open-ended tasks and projects

103. **What does critical thinking help students achieve?**

a) Memorize facts for exams

b) Analyze information to make reasoned decisions

c) Avoid complex topics

d) Complete tasks without reflection

Answer: b) Analyze information to make reasoned decisions

104. **Which strategy fosters student engagement in learning?**

a) Providing meaningful tasks that relate to real-life situations

b) Assigning repetitive worksheets

c) Delivering long lectures without breaks

d) Giving only written tests for assessment

Answer: a) Providing meaningful tasks that relate to real-life situations

105. **What is the role of reflection in learning?**

a) To enhance students' understanding of their learning process

b) To eliminate mistakes

c) To replace assessments

d) To provide only grades

Answer: a) To enhance students' understanding of their learning process

106**. How can teachers help students become independent learners?**

a) By promoting self-assessment and goal-setting

b) By providing answers to all questions

c) By giving only group tasks

d) By avoiding feedback on their work

Answer: a) By promoting self-assessment and goal-setting

107. **What is the primary purpose of diagnostic assessment?**

a) To identify students' strengths and areas for improvement

b) To assign final grades

c) To measure only attendance

d) To conduct national-level assessments

Answer: a) To identify students' strengths and areas for improvement

108. **Which of the following supports inclusive education?**

a) Providing equal opportunities for all students

b) Separating students by ability levels

c) Focusing only on academic performance

d) Ignoring students with special needs

Answer: a) Providing equal opportunities for all students

109. **What is a crucial benefit of formative assessment?**

a) It provides ongoing feedback to improve learning

b) It only measures students' final performance

c) It is conducted once a year

d) It eliminates the need for exams

Answer: a) It provides ongoing feedback to improve learning

110. **What is the purpose of peer assessment?**

a) To encourage collaboration and self-reflection among students

b) To replace teacher evaluation entirely

c) To create competition between students

d) To assign final grades

Answer: a) To encourage collaboration and self-reflection among students

111. **How can teachers address students' alternative conceptions?**

a) By exploring students' ideas and guiding them toward correct understanding

b) By ignoring misconceptions

c) By avoiding discussions on complex topics

d) By focusing only on textbook definitions

Answer: a) By exploring students' ideas and guiding them toward correct understanding

112. **What is the benefit of differentiated instruction?**

a) It meets the diverse learning needs of students

b) It treats all students the same

c) It limits student participation

d) It focuses only on high-achieving students

Answer: a) It meets the diverse learning needs of students

113. **Which activity promotes problem-solving skills?**

a) Working on hands-on projects

b) Memorizing textbook chapters

c) Copying notes without discussion

d) Taking only multiple-choice quizzes

Answer: a) Working on hands-on projects

114. **How can teachers support students with learning difficulties?**

a) By providing individualised support and extra resources

b) By assigning them more manageable tasks without challenges

c) By excluding them from group activities

d) By ignoring their needs

Answer: a) By providing individualised support and extra resources

115. **What type of motivation is driven by internal rewards and personal satisfaction?**

a) Intrinsic motivation

b) Extrinsic motivation

c) Social motivation

d) Competitive motivation

Answer: a) Intrinsic motivation

116. **How can teachers foster intrinsic motivation in students?**

a) By creating engaging and meaningful tasks

b) By offering only rewards and prizes

c) By comparing students to one another

d) By assigning repetitive tasks

Answer: a) By creating engaging and meaningful tasks

117. **What is an essential aspect of effective classroom management?**

a) Establishing clear expectations and rules

b) Ignoring disruptive behaviour

c) Focusing only on academic tasks

d) Limiting student interaction

Answer: a) Establishing clear expectations and rules

118. **How can teachers create a positive learning environment?**

a) By building supportive relationships with students

b) By focusing only on strict discipline

c) By reducing student participation

d) By eliminating classroom discussions

Answer: a) By building supportive relationships with students

119. **What is a crucial principle of constructivist learning theory?**

a) Learning occurs through active exploration and experience

b) Learning is passive and teacher-directed

c) Knowledge is transmitted directly from teacher to student

d) Students learn best through memorisation

Answer: a) Learning occurs through active exploration and experience

120. **How does emotional intelligence benefit students?**

a) It helps them manage their emotions and build positive relationships

b) It only improves academic performance

c) It eliminates the need for problem-solving

d) It limits creativity and self-awareness

Answer: a) It helps them manage their emotions and build positive relationships

121. **What does Vygotsky's concept of the Zone of Proximal Development (ZPD) describe?**

a) The gap between what a learner can do independently and with guidance

b) The ability to solve problems without help

c) Tasks that are too easy for the learner

d) The student's final level of achievement

Answer: a) The gap between what a learner can do independently and with guidance

122. **How can teachers apply Vygotsky's theory in the classroom?**

a) By providing guidance and support when needed

b) By giving students only independent tasks

c) By discouraging collaboration

d) By focusing only on memorisation tasks

Answer: a) By providing guidance and support when needed

123. **What is the purpose of project-based learning?**

a) To apply knowledge to solve real-world problems

b) To focus only on theory

c) To replace teamwork with individual work

d) To limit student creativity

Answer: a) To apply knowledge to solve real-world problems

124. **How can teachers help students develop a growth mindset?**

a) By praising effort and progress

b) By focusing only on the final results

c) By avoiding challenging tasks

d) By limiting feedback

Answer: a) By praising effort and progress

125. **What is the role of feedback in learning?**

a) To guide improvement

b) To assign final grades only

c) To discourage student questions

d) To eliminate reflection on mistakes

Answer: a) To guide improvement

126. What is the primary role of summative assessment?
a) To provide ongoing feedback during the learning
b) To evaluate overall learning at the end of a unit or course
c) To replace classroom activities with tests
d) To discourage collaborative learning
Answer: b) To evaluate overall learning at the end of a unit or course

127. What does formative assessment focus on?
a) Ranking students based on performance
b) Providing feedback to improve learning
c) Assigning final grades without feedback
d) Conducting tests only at the end of the course
Answer: b) Providing feedback to improve learning

128. Which of the following is a tool used in self-assessment?
a) Peer reviews
b) Portfolios
c) Standardized tests
d) End-of-term exams
Answer: b) Portfolios

129. What is the primary goal of continuous and comprehensive evaluation (CCE)?
a) To focus only on academic results
b) To assess both academic and non-academic areas regularly
c) To replace formative assessments
d) To conduct only final exams
Answer: b) To assess both academic and non-academic areas regularly

130.Which strategy promotes inclusion in the classroom?
a) Providing students with diverse abilities equal opportunities to participate
b) Grouping students by their performance levels
c) Ignoring students' individual learning needs

d) Assigning easier tasks to struggling students without support
Answer: a) Providing students with diverse abilities equal opportunities to participate

131. What does differentiated instruction mean?
a) Using the same teaching approach for all students
b) Tailoring teaching strategies to meet individual students' needs
c) Avoiding flexibility in teaching methods
d) Limiting lesson planning to one teaching style
Answer: b) Tailoring teaching strategies to meet individual students' needs

132. Which of the following describes peer learning?
a) Students competing for grades
b) Students teaching and learning from one another
c) Teachers delivering lectures without interaction
d) Group activities without shared learning
Answer: b) Students teaching and learning from one another

133. How can teachers encourage collaborative learning?
a) By assigning group projects and promoting teamwork
b) By focusing solely on individual assessments
c) By discouraging students from sharing ideas
d) By assigning only textbook-based tasks
Answer: a) By assigning group projects and promoting teamwork

134. What is an example of intrinsic motivation?
a) A student working hard to earn a reward
b) A student studying because they enjoy learning the subject
c) A student completing assignments to avoid punishment
d) A student performing well to get praise
Answer: b) A student studying because they enjoy learning the subject

135. Which theory suggests that students learn best when they actively construct their own understanding?
a) Behaviorism
b) Constructivism
c) Classical conditioning
d) Cognitive-behavioral theory
Answer: b) Constructivism

136. Which type of intelligence involves the ability to recognize and understand nature?
a) Linguistic intelligence
b) Logical-mathematical intelligence
c) Musical intelligence
d) Naturalistic intelligence
Answer: d) Naturalistic intelligence

137.How does emotional intelligence benefit students?
a) It helps them manage their emotions and build positive relationships
b) It reduces their need for social interaction
c) It only affects academic performance
d) It limits their participation in classroom activities
Answer: a) It helps them manage their emotions and build positive relationships

138.What does Vygotsky's theory emphasize about learning?
a) Learning is a social process
b) Learning occurs only through memorization
c) Students learn best through competition
d) Social interaction has little impact on learning
Answer: a) Learning is a social process

139.What is the role of feedback in peer assessment?
a) To discourage participation
b) To help students reflect and improve
c) To assign final grades
d) To replace teacher evaluations
Answer: b) To help students reflect and improve

140.What is one way teachers can address students' alternative conceptions?
a) By ignoring incorrect ideas
b) By exploring students' misconceptions and guiding them to correct understanding
c) By avoiding difficult topics
d) By giving students the correct answers immediately
Answer: b) By exploring students' misconceptions and guiding them to correct understanding

141.What is the purpose of project-based learning?
a) To promote real-world problem-solving skills
b) To focus only on theory
c) To limit teamwork and creativity
d) To replace all classroom activities with tests
Answer: a) To promote real-world problem-solving skills

142.Which strategy helps students develop critical thinking?
a) Memorizing textbook answers
b) Engaging in debates and discussions
c) Avoiding challenging topics
d) Limiting questions in class
Answer: b) Engaging in debates and discussions

143.How does collaborative learning benefit students?
a) It promotes teamwork and enhances social skills
b) It limits students' ability to think independently

c) It creates unnecessary competition
d) It discourages sharing of ideas
Answer: a) It promotes teamwork and enhances social skills

144.What does the Zone of Proximal Development (ZPD) describe?
a) Tasks a student can complete independently
b) The gap between what a student can do alone and what they can do with guidance
c) Activities that are too easy for a student
d) The final level of achievement in a subject
Answer: b) The gap between what a student can do alone and what they can do with guidance

145.How can teachers apply the concept of ZPD in the classroom?
a) By offering tasks that challenge students just beyond their current abilities
b) By assigning only easy tasks
c) By discouraging group work
d) By avoiding feedback and support
Answer: a) By offering tasks that challenge students just beyond their current abilities

146.How can teachers foster a growth mindset in students?
a) By praising effort and resilience
b) By focusing only on perfect results
c) By avoiding challenging tasks
d) By discouraging questions and feedback
Answer: a) By praising effort and resilience

147.What is the purpose of reflection in learning?
a) To help students analyze their learning experiences
b) To avoid mistakes in the future
c) To replace assessments
d) To discourage independent thinking
Answer: a) To help students analyze their learning experiences

148.How can self-assessment benefit students?
a) By encouraging them to take ownership of their learning
b) By reducing the need for teacher feedback
c) By focusing only on grades
d) By discouraging reflection
Answer: a) By encouraging them to take ownership of their learning

149.What role does motivation play in learning?
a) It has no impact on student achievement
b) It helps students stay engaged and persistent in their tasks
c) It only affects high-achieving students
d) It eliminates the need for feedback
Answer: b) It helps students stay engaged and persistent in their tasks

150.How can teachers create a positive classroom environment?
a) By building trust and fostering respect among students
b) By focusing only on discipline
c) By avoiding discussions and debates
d) By limiting student interaction
Answer: a) By building trust and fostering respect among students

151.What is extrinsic motivation driven by?
a) Personal curiosity
b) External rewards or recognition
c) The joy of learning itself
d) Involvement in personal interests
Answer: b) External rewards or recognition

152.How can teachers foster intrinsic motivation?
a) By giving frequent prizes
b) By creating meaningful learning experiences
c) By focusing only on grades
d) By limiting feedback
Answer: b) By creating meaningful learning experiences

153.What is the main goal of inclusive education?
a) To group students based on ability
b) To integrate all students, regardless of abilities, into the classroom
c) To focus only on students with disabilities
d) To reduce participation for struggling learners
Answer: b) To integrate all students, regardless of abilities, into the classroom

154.How can teachers support students with special needs?
a) By providing differentiated instruction
b) By ignoring their individual needs
c) By separating them from their peers
d) By assigning only basic tasks
Answer: a) By providing differentiated instruction

155.What is an example of differentiated instruction?
a) Using one method for all students
b) Modifying lessons based on students' needs and strengths
c) Assigning the same worksheet to every student
d) Teaching without considering individual differences
Answer: b) Modifying lessons based on students' needs and strengths

156.What does formative assessment focus on?
a) Monitoring progress and providing feedback during the learning process
b) Conducting final exams

c) Comparing students to each other
d) Ranking students based on performance
Answer: a) Monitoring progress and providing feedback during the learning process

157.What is the primary characteristic of summative assessment?
a) Ongoing feedback
b) End-of-course evaluation
c) Peer collaboration
d) Reflective learning
Answer: b) End-of-course evaluation

158.How does peer learning benefit students?
a) It fosters collaboration and builds teamwork
b) It discourages participation
c) It replaces teacher-led instruction
d) It promotes competition over cooperation
Answer: a) It fosters collaboration and builds teamwork

159.What role does feedback play in self-assessment?
a) It helps students identify areas for improvement
b) It eliminates the need for further learning
c) It only focuses on grades
d) It discourages independent learning
Answer: a) It helps students identify areas for improvement

160.Which teaching method promotes critical thinking?
a) Inquiry-based learning
b) Rote memorization
c) Lecture-based instruction
d) Multiple-choice quizzes only
Answer: a) Inquiry-based learning

161.What is the primary goal of project-based learning?
a) To solve real-world problems through hands-on activities
b) To focus only on theory
c) To eliminate teamwork
d) To discourage creativity
Answer: a) To solve real-world problems through hands-on activities

162.How does emotional intelligence support learning?
a) It helps students manage emotions and build relationships
b) It reduces academic performance
c) It discourages social interaction
d) It eliminates the need for collaboration
Answer: a) It helps students manage emotions and build relationships

163.What is the role of reflection in learning?
a) To enhance understanding through self-analysis
b) To focus solely on correct answers
c) To eliminate the need for feedback
d) To reduce engagement with the material
Answer: a) To enhance understanding through self-analysis

164.Which strategy promotes collaboration among students?
a) Group projects and discussions
b) Independent study only
c) Memorization without interaction
d) Avoiding teamwork
Answer: a) Group projects and discussions

165.How can teachers promote a growth mindset in students?
a) By praising effort and progress
b) By focusing only on outcomes
c) By discouraging challenges
d) By avoiding difficult tasks
Answer: a) By praising effort and progress

166.What is the purpose of diagnostic assessment?
a) To identify learning gaps and strengths early on
b) To assign grades at the end of the course
c) To provide continuous feedback
d) To rank students
Answer: a) To identify learning gaps and strengths early on

167.How can teachers create an inclusive learning environment?
a) By fostering respect and collaboration among all students
b) By focusing only on high achievers
c) By limiting participation for students with special needs
d) By assigning the same tasks to everyone
Answer: a) By fostering respect and collaboration among all students

168.Which type of motivation comes from personal satisfaction?
a) Intrinsic motivation
b) Extrinsic motivation
c) Social motivation
d) Competitive motivation
Answer: a) Intrinsic motivation

169.How can teachers apply Vygotsky's Zone of Proximal Development (ZPD)?
a) By offering tasks that students can complete with guidance
b) By assigning only easy tasks

c) By focusing only on independent activities
d) By avoiding group work
Answer: a) By offering tasks that students can complete with guidance

170.What is the main focus of school-based assessment?
a) Monitoring and evaluating learning throughout the year
b) Conducting exams at the national level
c) Comparing students with others in the same region
d) Eliminating classroom assessments
Answer: a) Monitoring and evaluating learning throughout the year

171.How can teachers promote independent learning?
a) By encouraging self-assessment and goal-setting
b) By limiting feedback
c) By focusing only on group activities
d) By discouraging student reflection
Answer: a) By encouraging self-assessment and goal-setting

172.What is an effective way to address students' misconceptions?
a) By discussing and correcting misunderstandings
b) By ignoring incorrect ideas
c) By providing answers without explanation
d) By avoiding difficult topics
Answer: a) By discussing and correcting misunderstandings

173.What role does feedback play in peer assessment?
a) It promotes reflection and improvement
b) It reduces collaboration
c) It focuses only on grades
d) It eliminates the need for self-assessment
Answer: a) It promotes reflection and improvement

174.How can teachers support students from diverse backgrounds?
a) By providing culturally relevant materials and activities
b) By focusing only on the dominant culture
c) By limiting discussions on diversity
d) By assigning the same resources to all students
Answer: a) By providing culturally relevant materials and activities

175.How does collaborative learning enhance problem-solving skills?
a) It encourages students to work together and share ideas
b) It limits creativity
c) It focuses only on individual performance
d) It discourages teamwork
Answer: a) It encourages students to work together and share ideas

176.How does formative assessment benefit students?
a) It provides immediate feedback for improvement
b) It only assigns final grades
c) It focuses solely on competitive exams
d) It eliminates the need for reflection
Answer: a) It provides immediate feedback for improvement

177.Which of the following best describes peer learning?
a) Students working together to teach and learn from each other
b) Students competing against each other
c) A teacher-led activity with no student interaction
d) Group work without collaboration
Answer: a) Students working together to teach and learn from each other

178.What is the purpose of summative assessment?
a) To evaluate students' overall learning at the end of a course
b) To monitor progress continuously
c) To replace formative assessments
d) To eliminate classroom discussions
Answer: a) To evaluate students' overall learning at the end of a course

179.How can teachers promote creativity in the classroom?
a) By encouraging open-ended projects and discussions
b) By focusing only on multiple-choice tests
c) By discouraging new ideas
d) By limiting group work
Answer: a) By encouraging open-ended projects and discussions

180.Which learning theory emphasizes social interaction in cognitive development?
a) Vygotsky's social development theory
b) Piaget's stages of development
c) Behaviorism
d) Classical conditioning
Answer: a) Vygotsky's social development theory

181.How can teachers foster a positive learning environment?
a) By building supportive relationships with students
b) By focusing only on academic tasks
c) By discouraging discussions
d) By limiting classroom participation
Answer: a) By building supportive relationships with students

182.What role does intrinsic motivation play in learning?
a) It encourages students to learn for personal satisfaction
b) It depends on external rewards

c) It eliminates the need for effort
d) It only benefits high achievers
Answer: a) It encourages students to learn for personal satisfaction

183. What is the main focus of project-based learning?
a) To engage students in real-world problem solving
b) To prioritize memorization
c) To limit teamwork
d) To focus only on theory
Answer: a) To engage students in real-world problem solving

184. Which of the following promotes emotional intelligence in students?
a) Teaching students to manage their emotions and empathize with others
b) Focusing only on academic skills
c) Avoiding emotional topics
d) Eliminating discussions about feelings
Answer: a) Teaching students to manage their emotions and empathize with others

185. What is the Zone of Proximal Development (ZPD)?
a) The difference between what a learner can do independently and with guidance
b) Tasks that are too easy for a student
c) Activities that require no support
d) The student's overall ability level
Answer: a) The difference between what a learner can do independently and with guidance

186. How can teachers promote collaborative learning?
a) By assigning tasks that require teamwork and group discussion
b) By encouraging only individual activities
c) By discouraging peer interaction
d) By limiting cooperative tasks
Answer: a) By assigning tasks that require teamwork and group discussion

187. What is the purpose of differentiated instruction?
a) To meet the diverse needs of all learners
b) To treat all students the same way
c) To focus only on high achievers
d) To simplify lessons for all students
Answer: a) To meet the diverse needs of all learners

188. Which assessment method encourages students to reflect on their progress?
a) Self-assessment
b) Standardized testing
c) Final exams
d) Aptitude tests
Answer: a) Self-assessment

189.How can teachers encourage critical thinking?
a) By asking open-ended questions and promoting debate
b) By discouraging discussions
c) By focusing only on textbook memorization
d) By giving students all the answers
Answer: a) By asking open-ended questions and promoting debate

190.What is the primary focus of Continuous and Comprehensive Evaluation (CCE)?
a) To assess both academic and non-academic areas regularly
b) To eliminate formative assessments
c) To conduct only standardized exams
d) To avoid feedback
Answer: a) To assess both academic and non-academic areas regularly

191.How does peer assessment benefit students?
a) It promotes collaboration and self-reflection
b) It reduces participation in the classroom
c) It eliminates the need for teacher feedback
d) It focuses only on final grades
Answer: a) It promotes collaboration and self-reflection

192.What is the role of reflection in learning?
a) To analyze personal experiences and improve learning
b) To reduce classroom participation
c) To assign final grades
d) To replace collaborative learning
Answer: a) To analyze personal experiences and improve learning

193.How can teachers apply constructivist learning in the classroom?
a) By encouraging students to explore and build their own understanding
b) By focusing only on lectures
c) By discouraging independent thought
d) By limiting student questions
Answer: a) By encouraging students to explore and build their own understanding

194.Which of the following best defines emotional intelligence?
a) The ability to manage one's emotions and understand others' emotions
b) Intelligence measured by IQ tests
c) The ability to solve mathematical problems
d) The ability to memorize information quickly
Answer: a) The ability to manage one's emotions and understand others' emotions

195.What is an Individualized Education Plan (IEP)?
a) A personalized plan designed to meet a student's specific learning needs
b) A general curriculum for all students

c) A behavior management tool
d) A list of classroom rules
Answer: a) A personalized plan designed to meet a student's specific learning needs

196.How can teachers foster independent learning?
a) By encouraging students to set goals and self-assess their progress
b) By providing all the answers
c) By focusing only on group tasks
d) By avoiding personal feedback
Answer: a) By encouraging students to set goals and self-assess their progress

197.What does collaborative learning encourage?
a) Teamwork and sharing of ideas
b) Competition among students
c) Memorization without interaction
d) Individual activities only
Answer: a) Teamwork and sharing of ideas

198.How can teachers create an inclusive classroom environment?
a) By fostering respect and valuing diversity
b) By ignoring individual differences
c) By assigning the same tasks to everyone
d) By focusing only on high performers
Answer: a) By fostering respect and valuing diversity

199.Which teaching strategy promotes problem-solving?
a) Inquiry-based learning
b) Memorization of facts
c) Multiple-choice tests only
d) Avoiding group discussions
Answer: a) Inquiry-based learning

200.What is a benefit of project-based learning?
a) It develops critical thinking and real-world problem-solving skills
b) It limits creativity
c) It focuses only on memorization
d) It discourages collaboration
Answer: a) It develops critical thinking and real-world problem-solving skills

Chapter 3: Questions

201.How does self-assessment benefit students?
a) It encourages them to take ownership of their learning
b) It eliminates the need for teacher feedback
c) It reduces classroom participation
d) It focuses only on final grades
Answer: a) It encourages them to take ownership of their learning

202.What role does motivation play in learning?
a) It helps students stay engaged and persistent in their tasks
b) It reduces student participation
c) It eliminates the need for effort
d) It only benefits high achievers
Answer: a) It helps students stay engaged and persistent in their tasks

203.How can teachers foster a growth mindset in students?
a) By praising effort and progress
b) By focusing only on correct answers
c) By avoiding challenging tasks
d) By discouraging student questions
Answer: a) By praising effort and progress

204.What is the primary characteristic of intrinsic motivation?
a) Learning for personal satisfaction and curiosity
b) Learning to earn rewards and prizes
c) Learning out of fear of punishment
d) Learning to compete with peers
Answer: a) Learning for personal satisfaction and curiosity

205.How can teachers encourage creativity among students?
a) By offering open-ended tasks and projects
b) By discouraging brainstorming
c) By focusing only on textbook-based learning
d) By limiting students to predefined solutions
Answer: a) By offering open-ended tasks and projects

206.What does emotional intelligence involve?
a) Managing one's emotions and understanding others' feelings
b) Scoring well on IQ tests
c) Memorizing emotional vocabulary
d) Avoiding emotional situations
Answer: a) Managing one's emotions and understanding others' feelings

207.How does collaborative learning enhance problem-solving skills?
a) By encouraging teamwork and sharing ideas
b) By focusing only on individual performance
c) By eliminating group activities
d) By promoting competition over cooperation
Answer: a) By encouraging teamwork and sharing ideas

208.Which strategy supports inclusive education?
a) Fostering respect and collaboration among students
b) Grouping students by their performance levels
c) Ignoring the needs of struggling learners
d) Assigning identical tasks to all students
Answer: a) Fostering respect and collaboration among students

209.How does project-based learning benefit students?
a) It promotes critical thinking and real-world problem solving
b) It focuses only on memorization
c) It discourages teamwork
d) It limits student creativity
Answer: a) It promotes critical thinking and real-world problem solving

210.What is the role of feedback in formative assessment?
a) To help students improve their learning
b) To rank students based on performance
c) To replace collaborative activities
d) To assign final grades
Answer: a) To help students improve their learning

211.What is the focus of Continuous and Comprehensive Evaluation (CCE)?
a) Assessing both academic and non-academic aspects
b) Conducting only final exams
c) Focusing on grades without feedback
d) Comparing students with national averages
Answer: a) Assessing both academic and non-academic aspects

212.How can teachers apply Vygotsky's theory in the classroom?
a) By providing tasks that require social interaction and guidance
b) By assigning only individual tasks
c) By avoiding peer collaboration
d) By focusing solely on memorization
Answer: a) By providing tasks that require social interaction and guidance

213.What does differentiated instruction aim to achieve?
a) Meeting the diverse needs of all students
b) Treating all students identically

c) Assigning only easy tasks
d) Avoiding personalized learning
Answer: a) Meeting the diverse needs of all students

214.How does peer learning benefit students?
a) It promotes collaboration and builds teamwork
b) It limits social interaction
c) It discourages student engagement
d) It focuses only on individual tasks
Answer: a) It promotes collaboration and builds teamwork

215.How can teachers promote critical thinking?
a) By encouraging debate and open-ended questions
b) By focusing only on textbook answers
c) By discouraging independent thought
d) By avoiding challenging topics
Answer: a) By encouraging debate and open-ended questions

216.What is a key benefit of inclusive education?
a) It ensures that students of all abilities learn together
b) It limits opportunities for struggling learners
c) It focuses only on academic success
d) It reduces participation in group activities
Answer: a) It ensures that students of all abilities learn together

217.How can teachers help students develop self-regulation skills?
a) By teaching goal-setting and time management
b) By eliminating deadlines
c) By focusing only on classroom rules
d) By discouraging independent planning
Answer: a) By teaching goal-setting and time management

218.What does formative assessment help teachers do?
a) Adjust instruction based on student progress
b) Assign grades without feedback
c) Eliminate classroom activities
d) Conduct only standardized exams
Answer: a) Adjust instruction based on student progress

219.How can reflection enhance learning?
a) By helping students analyze their experiences and improve
b) By focusing only on grades
c) By limiting creative tasks
d) By avoiding personal feedback
Answer: a) By helping students analyze their experiences and improve

220.What is a major goal of project-based learning?
a) To solve real-world problems through collaboration
b) To focus only on theory
c) To discourage teamwork
d) To promote individual performance exclusively
Answer: a) To solve real-world problems through collaboration

221.How can teachers foster motivation in students?
a) By creating meaningful and engaging tasks
b) By focusing only on external rewards
c) By ignoring student interests
d) By discouraging participation
Answer: a) By creating meaningful and engaging tasks

222.What role does emotional intelligence play in learning?
a) It enhances students' ability to manage emotions and build positive relationships
b) It focuses only on academic success
c) It discourages student interaction
d) It eliminates the need for collaboration
Answer: a) It enhances students' ability to manage emotions and build positive relationships

223.How can teachers promote problem-solving skills?
a) By encouraging exploration and inquiry
b) By focusing only on correct answers
c) By discouraging creative tasks
d) By limiting group work
Answer: a) By encouraging exploration and inquiry

224.What is the main focus of self-assessment?
a) Reflecting on progress to improve learning
b) Assigning final grades
c) Comparing scores with peers
d) Eliminating personal reflection
Answer: a) Reflecting on progress to improve learning

225. What does peer assessment encourage?
a) Collaboration and critical reflection
b) Competition among students
c) Avoidance of teamwork
d) Replacement of teacher feedback
Answer: a) Collaboration and critical reflection

226. How does collaborative learning support cognitive development?
a) By fostering interaction and sharing diverse perspectives
b) By focusing only on individual learning

c) By limiting students to memorisation tasks
d) By discouraging teamwork
Answer: a) By fostering interaction and sharing diverse perspectives

227. What is the role of goal-setting in student motivation?
a) It helps students focus and track progress toward their achievements
b) It eliminates the need for feedback
c) It encourages competition among students
d) It replaces self-reflection activities
Answer: a) It helps students focus and track progress toward their achievements

228. How does emotional intelligence contribute to teamwork?
a) It helps students manage emotions and collaborate effectively
b) It discourages social interaction
c) It reduces the need for group activities
d) It limits problem-solving abilities
Answer: a) It helps students manage emotions and collaborate effectively

229. What is the focus of reflective learning?
a) Analyzing experiences to understand and improve performance
b) Memorizing information without reflection
c) Avoiding critical thinking tasks
d) Focusing only on correct answers
Answer: a) Analyzing experiences to understand and improve performance

230. Which method encourages students to become independent learners?
a) Self-assessment and goal-setting
b) Memorizing textbook answers
c) Relying only on teacher guidance
d) Avoiding personal reflection
Answer: a) Self-assessment and goal-setting

231. How can teachers promote inquiry-based learning?
a) By encouraging students to ask questions and explore solutions
b) By providing direct answers without discussion
c) By limiting student questions
d) By avoiding real-world applications
Answer: a) By encouraging students to ask questions and explore solutions

232. What is the benefit of using portfolios in assessment?
a) They showcase students' progress and learning over time
b) They replace classroom activities
c) They eliminate the need for teacher feedback
d) They only focus on test scores
Answer: a) They showcase students' progress and learning over time

233. What is the primary purpose of formative assessment?
a) To provide feedback that helps improve learning during the process
b) To assign final grades
c) To conduct national-level exams
d) To rank students based on performance
Answer: a) To provide feedback that helps improve learning during the process

234. How can teachers support students from diverse cultural backgrounds?
a) By integrating culturally relevant content into lessons
b) By focusing only on one cultural perspective
c) By ignoring cultural diversity
d) By assigning identical tasks to all students
Answer: a) By integrating culturally relevant content into lessons

235. What is a crucial feature of project-based learning?
a) Students work on real-world challenges to develop critical thinking skills
b) Students memorise textbook information
c) Students complete tasks without collaboration
d) Students rely only on teacher instruction
Answer: a) Students work on real-world challenges to develop critical thinking skills

236. What is the role of motivation in achieving academic goals?
a) It drives students to put in consistent effort toward success
b) It discourages persistence
c) It eliminates the need for feedback
d) It benefits only high achievers
Answer: a) It drives students to put in consistent effort toward success

237. How can teachers use scaffolding effectively?
a) By providing temporary support that is gradually removed as students gain independence
b) By giving students the answers directly
c) By limiting students to individual tasks
d) By avoiding collaborative activities
Answer: a) By providing temporary support that is gradually removed as students gain independence

238. Which of the following promotes emotional regulation in students?
a) Teaching them strategies to manage their emotions
b) Focusing only on academic content
c) Discouraging discussions about feelings
d) Avoiding social interaction
Answer: a) Teaching them strategies to manage their emotions

239. How can teachers create an inclusive learning environment?
a) By valuing diversity and fostering respect among all students
b) By focusing only on academic success

c) By grouping students based on ability
d) By discouraging collaborative learning
Answer: a) By valuing diversity and fostering respect among all students

240. What is the benefit of using open-ended questions in the classroom?
a) They encourage students to think critically and explore multiple solutions
b) They limit student engagement
c) They focus only on memorisation
d) They discourage creative thinking
Answer: a) They encourage students to think critically and explore multiple solutions

241. How can teachers encourage students to reflect on their learning?
a) By asking them to maintain learning journals or portfolios
b) By focusing only on grades
c) By avoiding personal feedback
d) By eliminating reflective tasks
Answer: a) By asking them to maintain learning journals or portfolios

242. Which of the following describes self-regulation in learning?
a) The ability to set goals, manage time, and monitor one's progress
b) The ability to memorise information quickly
c) Relying entirely on teacher instructions
d) Avoiding independent work
Answer: a) The ability to set goals, manage time, and monitor one's progress

243. What is the main focus of Continuous and Comprehensive Evaluation (CCE)?
a) Monitoring student performance in both academic and non-academic areas
b) Conducting only end-of-term exams
c) Eliminating classroom assessments
d) Comparing students to national averages
Answer: a) Monitoring student performance in both academic and non-academic areas

244. How does peer feedback enhance learning?
a) It encourages students to reflect on their performance and improve
b) It reduces collaboration
c) It replaces teacher guidance
d) It discourages personal reflection
Answer: a) It encourages students to reflect on their performance and improve

245. What is a crucial principle of constructivist learning theory?
a) Learning is an active process where students build their understanding
b) Learning occurs only through memorisation
c) Knowledge is transmitted directly from teacher to student
d) Students learn best through passive listening
Answer: a) Learning is an active process where students build their understanding

246. How does formative assessment differ from summative assessment?
a) It provides feedback during the learning process
b) It only evaluates learning at the end of a course
c) It focuses solely on final grades
d) It eliminates continuous feedback
Answer: a) It provides feedback during the learning process

247. How can teachers support students with learning difficulties?
a) By offering personalised strategies and resources
b) By assigning the same tasks without modification
c) By ignoring their individual needs
d) By avoiding extra support
Answer: a) By offering personalised strategies and resources

248. What is an example of an effective feedback strategy?
a) Providing constructive feedback that focuses on improvement
b) Focusing only on students' mistakes
c) Avoiding feedback altogether
d) Comparing students to one another
Answer: a) Providing constructive feedback that focuses on improvement

249. How can teachers build a positive relationship with students?
a) By showing empathy and understanding toward their challenges
b) By focusing only on academic content
c) By limiting personal interaction
d) By discouraging student participation
Answer: a) By showing empathy and understanding toward their challenges

250. What is the purpose of an Individualized Education Plan (IEP)?
a) To provide customised learning strategies for students with special needs
b) To replace the general curriculum
c) To eliminate group activities
d) To assign the same tasks to all students
Answer: a) To provide customised learning strategies for students with special needs

251. What is the benefit of using group projects in the classroom?
a) They promote teamwork and collaboration
b) They eliminate the need for reflection
c) They focus only on individual learning
d) They discourage creativity
Answer: a) They promote teamwork and collaboration

252. How can teachers use scaffolding to improve student learning?
a) By providing gradual support and reducing help as students progress
b) By giving students all answers immediately

c) By avoiding challenging tasks
d) By focusing only on independent learning
Answer: a) By providing gradual support and reducing help as students progress

253. What does an inclusive classroom aim to achieve?
a) Learning opportunities for all students, regardless of ability
b) Segregation of students by performance
c) A focus only on high achievers
d) Separate learning environments for struggling students
Answer: a) Learning opportunities for all students, regardless of ability

254. How does intrinsic motivation influence student behaviour?
a) It encourages students to engage in tasks for personal satisfaction
b) It relies only on external rewards
c) It discourages self-directed learning
d) It eliminates the need for classroom participation
Answer: a) It encourages students to engage in tasks for personal satisfaction

255. What is the role of continuous assessment?
a) To monitor progress regularly and provide feedback
b) To assign final grades only
c) To replace formative assessments
d) To avoid evaluating non-academic areas
Answer: a) To monitor progress regularly and provide feedback

256. How can teachers support emotional development in students?
a) By teaching them how to manage emotions and build positive relationships
b) By focusing only on academic content
c) By discouraging discussions about emotions
d) By eliminating social activities
Answer: a) By teaching them how to manage emotions and build positive relationships

257. What is the purpose of goal-setting in education?
a) To help students focus on their objectives and track progress
b) To reduce student engagement
c) To eliminate classroom discussions
d) To assign grades automatically
Answer: a) To help students focus on their objectives and track progress

258. Which strategy promotes problem-solving skills?
a) Encouraging exploration and experimentation
b) Providing only theoretical content
c) Assigning tasks without context
d) Discouraging group activities
Answer: a) Encouraging exploration and experimentation

259. How does peer feedback benefit learning?
a) It helps students reflect and make improvements
b) It eliminates the need for teacher feedback
c) It discourages collaboration
d) It focuses only on grades
Answer: a) It helps students reflect and make improvements

260. How can teachers promote a positive classroom environment?
a) By fostering trust and respect among students
b) By focusing only on discipline
c) By discouraging student interaction
d) By avoiding teamwork
Answer: a) By fostering trust and respect among students

261. What does Vygotsky's theory emphasise about learning?
a) Learning occurs through social interaction and guidance
b) Learning happens only through independent study
c) Memorization is the primary method of learning
d) Social interaction has no role in learning
Answer: a) Learning occurs through social interaction and guidance

262. Which teaching method aligns with constructivist learning theory?
a) Hands-on activities and exploration
b) Memorization without interaction
c) Lectures with no student involvement
d) Textbook-based learning only
Answer: a) Hands-on activities and exploration

263. What is the goal of self-assessment?
a) To help students reflect on their progress and set goals
b) To assign grades without feedback
c) To compare students' performance
d) To eliminate personal reflection
Answer: a) To help students reflect on their progress and set goals

264. How does differentiated instruction benefit learners?
a) It addresses the diverse needs of all students
b) It treats all students the same way
c) It focuses only on advanced learners
d) It eliminates individual support
Answer: a) It addresses the diverse needs of all students

265. What is the benefit of reflection in learning?
a) It allows students to analyse their experiences and improve
b) It focuses only on grades

c) It limits classroom participation
d) It discourages critical thinking
Answer: a) It allows students to analyse their experiences and improve

266. How can teachers apply the Zone of Proximal Development (ZPD) in the classroom?
a) By providing tasks that students can complete with some guidance
b) By assigning only easy tasks
c) By discouraging collaboration
d) By avoiding group work
Answer: a) By providing tasks that students can complete with some guidance

267. How does feedback enhance learning?
a) It provides students with guidance for improvement
b) It focuses only on errors
c) It replaces assessments
d) It eliminates personal reflection
Answer: a) It provides students with guidance for improvement

268. What role does emotional intelligence play in teamwork?
a) It helps students manage emotions and work effectively with others
b) It discourages collaboration
c) It focuses only on academic success
d) It reduces student participation
Answer: a) It helps students manage emotions and work effectively with others

269. What is the primary goal of project-based learning?
a) To engage students in solving real-world problems
b) To prioritise memorization
c) To discourage teamwork
d) To replace all theoretical learning
Answer: a) To engage students in solving real-world problems

270. How does continuous and comprehensive evaluation (CCE) support students?
a) It monitors both academic and non-academic progress
b) It eliminates classroom activities
c) It focuses only on test scores
d) It discourages student participation
Answer: a) It monitors both academic and non-academic progress

271. How can teachers promote independent learning?
a) By encouraging self-assessment and personal goal-setting
b) By eliminating individual tasks
c) By focusing only on group projects
d) By avoiding feedback
Answer: a) By encouraging self-assessment and personal goal-setting

272. What is an example of an effective collaboration strategy?
a) Assigning group projects that require teamwork and shared responsibility
b) Assigning individual tasks only
c) Avoiding peer interaction
d) Focusing only on competitive activities
Answer: a) Assigning group projects that require teamwork and shared responsibility

273. How can teachers support students with special needs in an inclusive classroom?
a) By providing individualised support and accommodations
b) By grouping them separately
c) By assigning the same tasks as everyone else without adjustments
d) By avoiding challenging activities
Answer: a) By providing individualised support and accommodations

274. What is the purpose of peer assessment?
a) To encourage collaboration and self-reflection
b) To replace teacher feedback
c) To create competition among students
d) To focus only on final grades
Answer: a) To encourage collaboration and self-reflection

275. What role does curiosity play in learning?
a) It drives students to explore and discover new knowledge
b) It discourages independent thinking
c) It limits creativity
d) It focuses only on memorisation
Answer: a) It drives students to explore and discover new knowledge

276. What is the benefit of using open-ended questions in assessments?
a) They encourage critical thinking and creativity
b) They limit student responses
c) They reduce engagement in the classroom
d) They focus only on memorisation
Answer: a) They encourage critical thinking and creativity

277. How can teachers use formative assessment effectively?
a) By providing regular feedback to help students improve
b) By focusing only on end-of-term exams
c) By assigning grades without feedback
d) By avoiding continuous monitoring
Answer: a) By providing regular feedback to help students improve

278. How does peer learning enhance understanding?
a) By encouraging students to explain concepts to one another
b) By focusing only on competition

c) By reducing collaboration in the classroom
d) By avoiding group discussions
Answer: a) By encouraging students to explain concepts to one another

279. What is the primary goal of self-assessment?
a) To help students reflect on their learning and progress
b) To compare students' performance with peers
c) To replace classroom participation
d) To assign final grades
Answer: a) To help students reflect on their learning and progress

280. How can teachers support emotional intelligence development?
a) By teaching students to recognise and manage their emotions
b) By avoiding emotional topics
c) By limiting group activities
d) By focusing only on academic subjects
Answer: a) By teaching students to recognise and manage their emotions

281. What is the primary characteristic of intrinsic motivation?
a) Engaging in activities for personal satisfaction
b) Performing tasks for external rewards only
c) Learning to compete with others
d) Focusing only on grades
Answer: a) Engaging in activities for personal satisfaction

282. How does project-based learning benefit students?
a) It helps them apply knowledge to real-world situations
b) It limits student participation
c) It discourages teamwork
d) It focuses only on theoretical concepts
Answer: a) It helps them apply knowledge to real-world situations

283. How can teachers promote independent thinking in students?
a) By encouraging exploration and inquiry
b) By providing all answers immediately
c) By focusing only on group tasks
d) By discouraging student questions
Answer: a) By encouraging exploration and inquiry

284. Which strategy fosters collaboration among students?
a) Group projects that require teamwork and discussion
b) Assigning individual assessments only
c) Limiting classroom interaction
d) Discouraging peer interaction
Answer: a) Group projects that require teamwork and discussion

285. What does Vygotsky's theory of learning emphasise?
a) The importance of social interaction and guidance
b) Learning through rote memorisation
c) Independent learning without support
d) Competition as the primary driver of learning
Answer: a) The importance of social interaction and guidance

286. How can teachers create an inclusive learning environment?
a) By fostering respect for diversity and encouraging participation
b) By focusing only on academic performance
c) By grouping students based on ability
d) By avoiding collaboration
Answer: a) By fostering respect for diversity and encouraging participation

287. What is the purpose of reflective learning?
a) To analyse personal experiences and improve performance
b) To memorise facts without understanding
c) To avoid critical thinking tasks
d) To focus only on grades
Answer: a) To analyse personal experiences and improve performance

288. How can teachers apply scaffolding in the classroom?
a) By providing support as needed and gradually reducing it
b) By avoiding challenging tasks
c) By limiting student interaction
d) By focusing only on independent learning
Answer: a) By providing support as needed and gradually reducing it

289. What role does feedback play in learning?
a) It guides students in improving their performance
b) It focuses only on errors
c) It discourages participation
d) It eliminates self-reflection
Answer: a) It guides students in improving their performance

290. How can teachers promote a growth mindset?
a) By praising effort and persistence
b) By focusing only on outcomes
c) By avoiding complex tasks
d) By discouraging questions
Answer: a) By praising effort and persistence

291. What is the purpose of project-based learning?
a) To solve real-world problems through collaboration
b) To focus only on theoretical concepts

c) To discourage teamwork
d) To limit critical thinking
Answer: a) To solve real-world problems through collaboration

292. How does emotional intelligence benefit students?
a) It helps them manage emotions and build positive relationships
b) It discourages teamwork
c) It focuses only on academic success
d) It eliminates classroom interaction
Answer: a) It helps them manage emotions and build positive relationships

293. What is the primary goal of continuous and comprehensive evaluation (CCE)?
a) To assess both academic and non-academic performance regularly
b) To conduct only final exams
c) To focus solely on academic performance
d) To avoid classroom assessments
Answer: a) To assess both academic and non-academic performance regularly

294. How can teachers use differentiated instruction?
a) By adapting teaching strategies to meet individual needs
b) By treating all students the same
c) By avoiding flexible teaching methods
d) By assigning identical tasks to everyone
Answer: a) By adapting teaching strategies to meet individual needs

295. What is the purpose of self-regulation in learning?
a) To help students set goals and monitor their progress independently
b) To focus only on external rewards
c) To eliminate personal responsibility
d) To replace teacher feedback
Answer: a) To help students set goals and monitor their progress independently

296. How can peer learning benefit students?
a) By fostering collaboration and shared understanding
b) By limiting student participation
c) By promoting competition over teamwork
d) By avoiding group discussions
Answer: a) By fostering collaboration and shared understanding

297. How does formative assessment improve student outcomes?
a) By providing timely feedback for improvement
b) By focusing only on end-of-term exams
c) By avoiding classroom interaction
d) By ranking students
Answer: a) By providing timely feedback for improvement

298. What is the role of reflection in project-based learning?
a) To analyse progress and identify areas for improvement
b) To memorise facts without understanding
c) To discourage participation
d) To replace collaboration
Answer: a) To analyse progress and identify areas for improvement

299. How can teachers support students with learning difficulties?
a) By offering personalised resources and strategies
b) By ignoring their individual needs
c) By assigning identical tasks without modification
d) By avoiding feedback
Answer: a) By offering personalised resources and strategies

300.What is a key feature of peer assessment?
a) It encourages collaboration and critical reflection
b) It eliminates teacher involvement
c) It focuses only on grades
d) It discourages teamwork
Answer: a) It encourages collaboration and critical reflection

Chapter 4: Questions

301.How can teachers foster intrinsic motivation in students?
a) By offering meaningful tasks aligned with students' interests
b) By relying only on external rewards
c) By assigning repetitive worksheets
d) By discouraging questions
Answer: a) By offering meaningful tasks aligned with students' interests

302.What role does curiosity play in learning?
a) It encourages students to explore and discover new ideas
b) It limits students to memorization tasks
c) It reduces engagement in lessons
d) It discourages independent thought
Answer: a) It encourages students to explore and discover new ideas

303.How does emotional intelligence enhance classroom interaction?
a) It helps students understand and manage emotions, promoting healthy relationships
b) It discourages collaboration among students
c) It focuses only on individual performance
d) It eliminates the need for teamwork
Answer: a) It helps students understand and manage emotions, promoting healthy relationships

304.What is the primary focus of peer learning?
a) Collaborative learning through shared knowledge and experiences
b) Individual work without group interaction
c) Competition between students
d) Memorization without application
Answer: a) Collaborative learning through shared knowledge and experiences

305.How does project-based learning impact student outcomes?
a) It encourages critical thinking and real-world problem-solving skills
b) It limits creative thinking
c) It focuses only on memorization
d) It discourages teamwork
Answer: a) It encourages critical thinking and real-world problem-solving skills

306.What is the purpose of formative assessment?
a) To provide feedback during the learning process for improvement
b) To replace summative assessments
c) To compare students with national standards
d) To assign final grades only
Answer: a) To provide feedback during the learning process for improvement

307.How does self-assessment benefit students?
a) It encourages them to reflect on their progress and set learning goals
b) It eliminates the need for feedback
c) It focuses only on grades
d) It discourages independent learning
Answer: a) It encourages them to reflect on their progress and set learning goals

308.What is a key characteristic of differentiated instruction?
a) Adapting teaching methods to meet the diverse needs of students
b) Treating all students the same way
c) Eliminating flexibility in teaching
d) Focusing only on high-achieving students
Answer: a) Adapting teaching methods to meet the diverse needs of students

309.How can teachers promote emotional well-being in the classroom?
a) By creating a supportive and respectful environment
b) By focusing only on academic content
c) By avoiding discussions about emotions
d) By limiting student interaction
Answer: a) By creating a supportive and respectful environment

310.What is the goal of the Zone of Proximal Development (ZPD)?
a) To provide tasks that students can complete with guidance
b) To focus only on independent learning
c) To assign only easy tasks
d) To eliminate collaboration
Answer: a) To provide tasks that students can complete with guidance

311.How does feedback enhance student performance?
a) By guiding students to improve and achieve their learning goals
b) By focusing only on mistakes
c) By discouraging participation
d) By avoiding constructive criticism
Answer: a) By guiding students to improve and achieve their learning goals

312.Which strategy fosters independent learning?
a) Encouraging self-assessment and personal reflection
b) Providing all answers to students
c) Avoiding student questions
d) Focusing only on group tasks
Answer: a) Encouraging self-assessment and personal reflection

313.What is the main benefit of project-based learning?
a) It helps students apply knowledge to real-world challenges
b) It reduces the need for practical activities

c) It focuses only on memorization
d) It discourages teamwork
Answer: a) It helps students apply knowledge to real-world challenges

314.How does continuous and comprehensive evaluation (CCE) support students?
a) By assessing both academic and non-academic areas regularly
b) By eliminating formative assessments
c) By focusing only on final exams
d) By discouraging feedback
Answer: a) By assessing both academic and non-academic areas regularly

315.What is the primary role of feedback in learning?
a) To provide guidance for improvement and encourage growth
b) To replace collaborative learning
c) To assign grades without reflection
d) To discourage student participation
Answer: a) To provide guidance for improvement and encourage growth

316.How can teachers encourage critical thinking?
a) By promoting inquiry and asking open-ended questions
b) By avoiding challenging topics
c) By focusing only on memorization
d) By limiting classroom discussions
Answer: a) By promoting inquiry and asking open-ended questions

317.How does intrinsic motivation benefit students?
a) It encourages them to learn for personal satisfaction and curiosity
b) It depends on rewards and recognition
c) It reduces engagement in the classroom
d) It discourages self-directed learning
Answer: a) It encourages them to learn for personal satisfaction and curiosity

318.What is the role of collaboration in problem-solving?
a) It fosters teamwork and encourages the sharing of ideas
b) It discourages student participation
c) It eliminates creativity
d) It focuses only on individual performance
Answer: a) It fosters teamwork and encourages the sharing of ideas

319.How can teachers support students with learning difficulties?
a) By providing personalized resources and strategies
b) By assigning the same tasks to all students
c) By avoiding feedback
d) By grouping them separately
Answer: a) By providing personalized resources and strategies

320.How does emotional intelligence influence teamwork?
a) It helps students manage emotions and work effectively with others
b) It discourages group activities
c) It focuses only on individual performance
d) It eliminates collaboration
Answer: a) It helps students manage emotions and work effectively with others

321.What is a key benefit of peer feedback?
a) It promotes reflection and encourages improvement
b) It focuses only on mistakes
c) It eliminates the need for teacher guidance
d) It discourages self-assessment
Answer: a) It promotes reflection and encourages improvement

322.How can teachers promote a growth mindset?
a) By encouraging students to embrace challenges and learn from failures
b) By focusing only on perfect outcomes
c) By discouraging questions
d) By avoiding feedback
Answer: a) By encouraging students to embrace challenges and learn from failures

323.What does differentiated instruction aim to achieve?
a) Meeting the diverse needs of all students
b) Treating all students the same way
c) Focusing only on advanced learners
d) Limiting classroom activities
Answer: a) Meeting the diverse needs of all students

324.What is the focus of reflective learning?
a) Analyzing experiences to improve future performance
b) Avoiding critical thinking tasks
c) Memorizing facts without reflection
d) Focusing only on correct answers
Answer: a) Analyzing experiences to improve future performance

325.How can teachers create a positive learning environment?
a) By fostering respect and building supportive relationships with students
b) By focusing only on discipline
c) By avoiding student interaction
d) By limiting collaboration
Answer: a) By fostering respect and building supportive relationships with students

26.What is the role of self-assessment in learning?
a) It helps students reflect on their progress and set goals
b) It eliminates the need for teacher feedback

c) It discourages reflection and growth
d) It focuses only on grades
Answer: a) It helps students reflect on their progress and set goals

327.How can teachers support independent learning?
a) By promoting goal-setting and self-monitoring strategies
b) By giving students answers directly
c) By avoiding feedback
d) By focusing only on group work
Answer: a) By promoting goal-setting and self-monitoring strategies

328.How does collaborative learning benefit students?
a) It fosters teamwork and enhances critical thinking
b) It discourages creativity
c) It focuses only on competition
d) It reduces engagement
Answer: a) It fosters teamwork and enhances critical thinking

329.What is the primary focus of intrinsic motivation?
a) Engaging in tasks for personal satisfaction and curiosity
b) Completing tasks only for rewards and recognition
c) Learning only to compete with peers
d) Focusing solely on grades
Answer: a) Engaging in tasks for personal satisfaction and curiosity

330.What is a key principle of project-based learning?
a) Solving real-world problems through hands-on activities
b) Memorizing facts without application
c) Avoiding group work
d) Focusing only on individual tasks
Answer: a) Solving real-world problems through hands-on activities

331.How does emotional intelligence support learning?
a) It helps students manage their emotions and build positive relationships
b) It reduces the need for interaction
c) It focuses only on academic performance
d) It discourages collaboration
Answer: a) It helps students manage their emotions and build positive relationships

332.What is the purpose of formative assessment?
a) To provide ongoing feedback for improvement during learning
b) To replace final exams
c) To focus only on assigning grades
d) To rank students based on performance
Answer: a) To provide ongoing feedback for improvement during learning

333.What role does feedback play in student learning?
a) It guides students toward improvement and helps them achieve their goals
b) It discourages participation in class
c) It eliminates the need for reflection
d) It focuses only on mistakes
Answer: a) It guides students toward improvement and helps them achieve their goals

334.How can teachers promote inquiry-based learning?
a) By encouraging students to ask questions and explore solutions
b) By limiting discussions and debates
c) By focusing only on memorization tasks
d) By providing answers without context
Answer: a) By encouraging students to ask questions and explore solutions

335.How does peer learning improve understanding?
a) By encouraging students to explain concepts to each other
b) By discouraging teamwork
c) By focusing only on competition
d) By avoiding group discussions
Answer: a) By encouraging students to explain concepts to each other

336.What is the benefit of differentiated instruction?
a) It addresses the individual needs of all students
b) It eliminates flexibility in teaching
c) It focuses only on high achievers
d) It discourages student participation
Answer: a) It addresses the individual needs of all students

337.How can teachers encourage students to become independent learners?
a) By promoting self-assessment and goal setting
b) By focusing only on teacher-led instruction
c) By discouraging independent exploration
d) By limiting student interaction
Answer: a) By promoting self-assessment and goal setting

338.What does reflective learning encourage?
a) Analyzing experiences to improve future performance
b) Avoiding critical thinking tasks
c) Memorizing facts without reflection
d) Focusing only on grades
Answer: a) Analyzing experiences to improve future performance

339.How can teachers foster a growth mindset?
a) By encouraging students to embrace challenges and learn from mistakes
b) By avoiding difficult tasks
c) By focusing only on final grades
d) By discouraging student questions
Answer: a) By encouraging students to embrace challenges and learn from mistakes

340.What is the focus of continuous and comprehensive evaluation (CCE)?
a) Assessing both academic and non-academic areas regularly
b) Conducting only final exams
c) Focusing only on academic performance
d) Avoiding formative assessments
Answer: a) Assessing both academic and non-academic areas regularly

341.How can teachers use scaffolding effectively?
a) By providing temporary support that gradually decreases as students gain independence
b) By avoiding support altogether
c) By focusing only on easy tasks
d) By eliminating group work
Answer: a) By providing temporary support that gradually decreases as students gain independence

342.What is the role of feedback in project-based learning?
a) It helps students analyze their progress and make improvements
b) It focuses only on final grades
c) It discourages teamwork
d) It replaces collaboration
Answer: a) It helps students analyze their progress and make improvements

343.How does emotional intelligence enhance teamwork?
a) It helps students manage their emotions and collaborate effectively
b) It reduces the need for interaction
c) It focuses only on individual performance
d) It eliminates collaboration
Answer: a) It helps students manage their emotions and collaborate effectively

344.What is a key feature of peer assessment?
a) It promotes reflection and encourages improvement
b) It eliminates the need for teacher feedback
c) It focuses only on mistakes
d) It discourages teamwork
Answer: a) It promotes reflection and encourages improvement

345.How does project-based learning engage students?
a) By providing real-world challenges that require critical thinking
b) By focusing only on textbook knowledge
c) By eliminating group activities
d) By discouraging creativity
Answer: a) By providing real-world challenges that require critical thinking

346.How can teachers create a positive learning environment?
a) By fostering trust, respect, and open communication
b) By focusing only on discipline
c) By avoiding interaction among students
d) By limiting collaborative activities
Answer: a) By fostering trust, respect, and open communication

347.What is the main purpose of formative assessment?
a) To provide feedback that improves learning during the process
b) To assign final grades only
c) To conduct national exams
d) To avoid monitoring student progress
Answer: a) To provide feedback that improves learning during the process

348.How can teachers support students with learning difficulties?
a) By offering individualized strategies and accommodations
b) By treating them the same as all other students
c) By assigning easier tasks without feedback
d) By avoiding additional support
Answer: a) By offering individualized strategies and accommodations

349.What is the goal of self-assessment?
a) To encourage students to reflect on their learning and set personal goals
b) To eliminate feedback from teachers
c) To focus only on grades
d) To discourage personal reflection
Answer: a) To encourage students to reflect on their learning and set personal goals

350.How can teachers promote independent learning?
a) By encouraging self-assessment and goal setting
b) By providing all the answers
c) By discouraging questions
d) By focusing only on group work
Answer: a) By encouraging self-assessment and goal setting

351.What is the benefit of using reflective journals in learning?
a) They encourage students to analyze their experiences and grow
b) They replace classroom discussions
c) They eliminate feedback from teachers
d) They discourage critical thinking
Answer: a) They encourage students to analyze their experiences and grow

352.How can teachers promote problem-solving skills?
a) By encouraging exploration and inquiry-based activities
b) By focusing only on memorization tasks
c) By providing direct answers without discussion
d) By discouraging group projects
Answer: a) By encouraging exploration and inquiry-based activities

353.What does peer learning foster?
a) Collaboration and shared responsibility
b) Competition among students
c) Avoidance of teamwork
d) Limited interaction between peers
Answer: a) Collaboration and shared responsibility

354.How can teachers create a growth mindset environment?
a) By praising effort and resilience
b) By focusing only on correct answers
c) By discouraging challenges
d) By eliminating feedback
Answer: a) By praising effort and resilience

355.What is the main focus of continuous assessment?
a) Monitoring student progress throughout the course
b) Conducting final exams only
c) Comparing students' results with others
d) Eliminating formative feedback
Answer: a) Monitoring student progress throughout the course

356.How can scaffolding support learning?
a) By gradually removing support as students gain competence
b) By giving students direct solutions
c) By discouraging independent thinking
d) By avoiding collaborative tasks
Answer: a) By gradually removing support as students gain competence

357.What is a key principle of constructivist learning theory?
a) Students build their own understanding through experiences
b) Knowledge is transmitted directly from teacher to student
c) Learning occurs only through repetition
d) Memorization is the primary learning method
Answer: a) Students build their own understanding through experiences

358.How can teachers support students with special needs?
a) By adapting lessons to meet individual needs
b) By giving them the same tasks as others without adjustments
c) By separating them from their peers
d) By avoiding feedback
Answer: a) By adapting lessons to meet individual needs

359.What is the role of feedback in self-assessment?
a) It guides students to reflect and improve their performance
b) It discourages personal reflection
c) It replaces all classroom assessments
d) It focuses only on grades
Answer: a) It guides students to reflect and improve their performance

360.What does collaborative learning encourage?
a) Teamwork and mutual understanding
b) Individual competition
c) Passive listening
d) Avoidance of group tasks
Answer: a) Teamwork and mutual understanding

361.How can teachers promote emotional intelligence?
a) By teaching students to manage emotions and empathize with others
b) By avoiding social interaction
c) By focusing only on academic performance
d) By discouraging teamwork
Answer: a) By teaching students to manage emotions and empathize with others

362.What is a key feature of formative assessment?
a) It provides feedback during learning to guide improvement
b) It focuses only on final grades
c) It eliminates continuous feedback
d) It ranks students based on their performance
Answer: a) It provides feedback during learning to guide improvement

363.What is the role of goal-setting in learning?
a) It helps students stay focused and track their progress
b) It discourages reflection
c) It focuses only on final outcomes
d) It limits student engagement
Answer: a) It helps students stay focused and track their progress

364.How can teachers encourage independent learning?
a) By promoting self-reflection and goal setting
b) By discouraging exploration
c) By providing all the answers
d) By limiting feedback
Answer: a) By promoting self-reflection and goal setting

365.What does reflective learning emphasize?
a) Analyzing experiences to improve future learning
b) Memorizing facts without understanding
c) Focusing only on grades
d) Avoiding critical thinking
Answer: a) Analyzing experiences to improve future learning

366.How can teachers support students from diverse backgrounds?
a) By incorporating culturally relevant content into lessons
b) By focusing only on one cultural perspective
c) By ignoring cultural diversity
d) By treating all students identically
Answer: a) By incorporating culturally relevant content into lessons

367.How does intrinsic motivation impact learning?
a) It drives students to learn for personal satisfaction
b) It relies solely on rewards and prizes
c) It discourages independent thought
d) It limits creativity
Answer: a) It drives students to learn for personal satisfaction

368.What is the primary goal of project-based learning?
a) To solve real-world problems through collaborative efforts
b) To focus only on memorization tasks
c) To eliminate teamwork
d) To discourage exploration
Answer: a) To solve real-world problems through collaborative efforts

369.How does peer feedback enhance learning?
a) It encourages students to reflect and improve based on peer input
b) It eliminates teacher involvement
c) It focuses only on grades
d) It discourages collaboration
Answer: a) It encourages students to reflect and improve based on peer input

370.What is the purpose of scaffolding in learning?
a) To provide temporary support until students gain independence
b) To give students all answers immediately
c) To avoid challenging tasks
d) To limit exploration
Answer: a) To provide temporary support until students gain independence

371.How can teachers build a positive classroom environment?
a) By fostering respect, empathy, and open communication
b) By focusing only on academic tasks
c) By discouraging interaction
d) By limiting feedback
Answer: a) By fostering respect, empathy, and open communication

372.What is the role of emotional intelligence in teamwork?
a) It helps students collaborate effectively by managing emotions
b) It discourages group participation
c) It focuses only on individual performance
d) It limits communication
Answer: a) It helps students collaborate effectively by managing emotions

373.How can teachers foster critical thinking?
a) By encouraging open-ended questions and inquiry
b) By focusing only on textbook answers
c) By discouraging debate
d) By avoiding challenging topics
Answer: a) By encouraging open-ended questions and inquiry

374.How does continuous and comprehensive evaluation (CCE) benefit students?
a) It monitors both academic and non-academic progress regularly
b) It eliminates feedback
c) It focuses only on final exams
d) It avoids evaluating social skills
Answer: a) It monitors both academic and non-academic progress regularly

375.How can teachers support students with learning challenges?
a) By providing personalized strategies and additional resources
b) By avoiding feedback
c) By treating all students identically
d) By excluding them from group activities
Answer: a) By providing personalized strategies and additional resources

376.How does goal-setting benefit students?
a) It helps them focus and track their progress toward achievements
b) It discourages independent thinking
c) It eliminates self-reflection
d) It limits classroom participation
Answer: a) It helps them focus and track their progress toward achievements

377.What is a key element of inquiry-based learning?
a) Encouraging students to ask questions and explore answers
b) Memorizing facts without critical thinking
c) Limiting student interaction
d) Providing all answers directly
Answer: a) Encouraging students to ask questions and explore answers

378.How can teachers promote collaboration in the classroom?
a) By assigning group tasks that require teamwork
b) By focusing only on individual assessments
c) By discouraging peer interaction
d) By eliminating group projects
Answer: a) By assigning group tasks that require teamwork

379.What is the main role of emotional intelligence in learning?
a) It helps students manage emotions and build positive relationships
b) It discourages interaction among students
c) It focuses only on academic tasks
d) It eliminates the need for teamwork
Answer: a) It helps students manage emotions and build positive relationships

380.How does project-based learning support student engagement?
a) It involves solving real-world challenges through teamwork
b) It limits participation to individual tasks
c) It discourages collaboration
d) It focuses only on memorization
Answer: a) It involves solving real-world challenges through teamwork

381.What is the purpose of self-assessment?
a) To encourage students to reflect on their learning and set goals
b) To replace classroom discussions

c) To assign final grades only
d) To focus only on comparing students
Answer: a) To encourage students to reflect on their learning and set goals

382.How can teachers promote a positive classroom environment?
a) By fostering respect, empathy, and trust
b) By focusing only on discipline
c) By avoiding student interaction
d) By discouraging participation
Answer: a) By fostering respect, empathy, and trust

383.What is a key feature of continuous assessment?
a) It monitors learning throughout the course and provides feedback
b) It focuses only on final exams
c) It eliminates formative evaluation
d) It limits interaction in the classroom
Answer: a) It monitors learning throughout the course and provides feedback

384.How can teachers support students with diverse needs?
a) By providing differentiated instruction and resources
b) By assigning identical tasks to all students
c) By avoiding feedback on performance
d) By separating students by ability
Answer: a) By providing differentiated instruction and resources

385.What is the benefit of reflective learning?
a) It helps students analyze their experiences and improve
b) It discourages personal reflection
c) It focuses only on grades
d) It eliminates critical thinking
Answer: a) It helps students analyze their experiences and improve

386.What is the role of peer feedback?
a) It promotes reflection and encourages improvement
b) It replaces teacher guidance entirely
c) It focuses only on final grades
d) It discourages teamwork
Answer: a) It promotes reflection and encourages improvement

387.How can teachers use scaffolding effectively?
a) By gradually reducing support as students become independent
b) By avoiding student questions
c) By providing direct answers only
d) By discouraging collaboration
Answer: a) By gradually reducing support as students become independent

388.How does emotional intelligence benefit teamwork?
a) It helps students collaborate by managing emotions and empathizing with others
b) It reduces student participation
c) It focuses only on academic performance
d) It eliminates group activities
Answer: a) It helps students collaborate by managing emotions and empathizing with others

389.What is the main focus of project-based learning?
a) Solving real-world problems through collaborative efforts
b) Memorizing textbook content
c) Avoiding teamwork
d) Replacing hands-on learning with theory
Answer: a) Solving real-world problems through collaborative efforts

390.How can teachers promote critical thinking?
a) By asking open-ended questions and encouraging debate
b) By discouraging challenging tasks
c) By focusing only on textbook answers
d) By limiting discussions
Answer: a) By asking open-ended questions and encouraging debate

391.What is the purpose of formative assessment?
a) To provide feedback during learning to improve performance
b) To assign final grades only
c) To eliminate continuous evaluation
d) To discourage participation
Answer: a) To provide feedback during learning to improve performance

392.How does continuous and comprehensive evaluation (CCE) support students?
a) It assesses both academic and non-academic progress regularly
b) It eliminates formative feedback
c) It focuses only on final exams
d) It discourages student reflection
Answer: a) It assesses both academic and non-academic progress regularly

393.How can teachers encourage self-directed learning?
a) By promoting self-assessment and goal setting
b) By providing all solutions directly
c) By discouraging independent thinking
d) By focusing only on group tasks
Answer: a) By promoting self-assessment and goal setting

394.What is the role of scaffolding in learning?
a) To provide temporary support until students become independent
b) To replace hands-on activities
c) To focus only on memorization
d) To eliminate student participation
Answer: a) To provide temporary support until students become independent

395.How can teachers support students from different cultural backgrounds?
a) By integrating culturally relevant content into lessons
b) By focusing only on one cultural perspective
c) By treating all students identically
d) By avoiding discussions about diversity
Answer: a) By integrating culturally relevant content into lessons

396.What is the benefit of project-based learning?
a) It promotes critical thinking and real-world problem solving
b) It eliminates teamwork
c) It focuses only on theory
d) It discourages creativity
Answer: a) It promotes critical thinking and real-world problem solving

397.How does emotional intelligence impact student success?
a) It helps students manage emotions and build positive relationships
b) It discourages collaboration
c) It focuses only on academic results
d) It limits student engagement
Answer: a) It helps students manage emotions and build positive relationships

398.How can teachers foster motivation in students?
a) By creating engaging and meaningful tasks
b) By focusing only on grades
c) By avoiding feedback
d) By discouraging participation
Answer: a) By creating engaging and meaningful tasks

399.What is the purpose of self-reflection in learning?
a) To analyze experiences and improve future performance
b) To focus only on final outcomes
c) To discourage independent thought
d) To avoid feedback
Answer: a) To analyze experiences and improve future performance

400.How can peer learning enhance student understanding?
a) By allowing students to teach and learn from each other
b) By discouraging interaction
c) By limiting collaborative tasks
d) By focusing only on individual work
Answer: a) By allowing students to teach and learn from each other

Chapter 5: Questions

401.How does formative assessment benefit students?
a) It provides feedback that helps improve learning during the process
b) It assigns final grades without feedback
c) It discourages student participation
d) It eliminates classroom interaction
Answer: a) It provides feedback that helps improve learning during the process

402.How can teachers promote problem-solving skills?
a) By encouraging students to explore multiple solutions
b) By providing direct answers to all questions
c) By focusing only on memorization
d) By discouraging discussions
Answer: a) By encouraging students to explore multiple solutions

403.What is a key benefit of peer learning?
a) It promotes collaborative learning and shared understanding
b) It discourages teamwork and interaction
c) It focuses only on competition
d) It limits student engagement
Answer: a) It promotes collaborative learning and shared understanding

404.How can teachers foster independent learning?
a) By encouraging goal setting and self-assessment
b) By limiting student autonomy
c) By discouraging reflection
d) By avoiding challenging tasks
Answer: a) By encouraging goal setting and self-assessment

405.What does continuous and comprehensive evaluation (CCE) monitor?
a) Both academic and non-academic progress regularly
b) Only final exam results
c) Only academic scores
d) Classroom behavior only
Answer: a) Both academic and non-academic progress regularly

406.How can teachers support emotional intelligence development?
a) By teaching students to recognize and manage their emotions
b) By ignoring social interaction
c) By focusing only on academics
d) By discouraging teamwork
Answer: a) By teaching students to recognize and manage their emotions

407.What is the purpose of scaffolding?
a) To provide temporary support and promote independent learning
b) To complete tasks for students
c) To avoid feedback
d) To limit student questions
Answer: a) To provide temporary support and promote independent learning

408.How does project-based learning promote engagement?
a) It involves solving real-world problems with collaboration
b) It discourages teamwork
c) It focuses only on memorization
d) It avoids practical activities
Answer: a) It involves solving real-world problems with collaboration

409.How can teachers create a growth mindset?
a) By encouraging students to embrace challenges and learn from mistakes
b) By focusing only on perfect results
c) By discouraging exploration
d) By limiting feedback
Answer: a) By encouraging students to embrace challenges and learn from mistakes

410.What is the benefit of reflective learning?
a) It helps students analyze experiences and improve their performance
b) It focuses only on memorization
c) It limits student interaction
d) It discourages critical thinking
Answer: a) It helps students analyze experiences and improve their performance

411.How can teachers support students with special needs?
a) By offering personalized strategies and accommodations
b) By assigning the same tasks to everyone
c) By avoiding group activities
d) By discouraging feedback
Answer: a) By offering personalized strategies and accommodations

412.What does self-assessment encourage?
a) Reflection on progress and setting learning goals
b) Avoidance of independent thinking
c) Focus only on grades
d) Memorization without understanding
Answer: a) Reflection on progress and setting learning goals

413.How does emotional intelligence benefit group work?
a) It helps students collaborate effectively by managing emotions

b) It discourages teamwork
c) It focuses only on academic performance
d) It eliminates peer interaction
Answer: a) It helps students collaborate effectively by managing emotions

414.How does peer feedback enhance learning?
a) It promotes reflection and improvement through peer input
b) It discourages self-assessment
c) It replaces teacher feedback entirely
d) It focuses only on grades
Answer: a) It promotes reflection and improvement through peer input

415.What is a key feature of inquiry-based learning?
a) Encouraging students to ask questions and find answers
b) Memorizing facts without discussion
c) Avoiding real-world applications
d) Limiting interaction between students
Answer: a) Encouraging students to ask questions and find answers

416.How can teachers foster collaboration?
a) By assigning tasks that require teamwork and group effort
b) By focusing only on individual tasks
c) By discouraging peer interaction
d) By avoiding group projects
Answer: a) By assigning tasks that require teamwork and group effort

417.What role does motivation play in learning?
a) It drives students to stay engaged and persistent in their efforts
b) It discourages student participation
c) It eliminates the need for feedback
d) It benefits only high achievers
Answer: a) It drives students to stay engaged and persistent in their efforts

418.How does scaffolding promote learning?
a) By gradually reducing support as students become more competent
b) By providing answers directly to students
c) By discouraging exploration
d) By avoiding complex tasks
Answer: a) By gradually reducing support as students become more competent

419.How can teachers promote problem-solving skills?
a) By encouraging students to experiment with different solutions
b) By focusing only on textbook answers
c) By avoiding group work
d) By discouraging questions
Answer: a) By encouraging students to experiment with different solutions

420.What is the purpose of continuous assessment?
a) To monitor learning and provide feedback throughout the course
b) To assign final grades only
c) To eliminate classroom assessments
d) To avoid evaluating non-academic progress
Answer: a) To monitor learning and provide feedback throughout the course

421.How does reflection benefit students?
a) It helps them analyze their experiences and improve
b) It discourages independent thought
c) It focuses only on grades
d) It limits creativity
Answer: a) It helps them analyze their experiences and improve

422.How can teachers support culturally diverse students?
a) By integrating culturally relevant content into lessons
b) By ignoring cultural differences
c) By treating all students the same way
d) By discouraging discussions about culture
Answer: a) By integrating culturally relevant content into lessons

423.What is the role of feedback in formative assessment?
a) To guide students in improving their learning during the process
b) To assign final grades without reflection
c) To discourage classroom interaction
d) To limit student participation
Answer: a) To guide students in improving their learning during the process

424.How can teachers promote independent learning?
a) By encouraging students to reflect on their progress and set goals
b) By providing all answers immediately
c) By discouraging exploration
d) By focusing only on group projects
Answer: a) By encouraging students to reflect on their progress and set goals

425.What is the benefit of project-based learning?
a) It encourages critical thinking and problem solving in real-world contexts

b) It focuses only on memorization
c) It eliminates the need for collaboration
d) It discourages teamwork
Answer: a) It encourages critical thinking and problem solving in real-world contexts

426.How can teachers encourage critical thinking?
a) By asking open-ended questions and encouraging debate
b) By discouraging exploration
c) By focusing only on rote learning
d) By limiting classroom discussions
Answer: a) By asking open-ended questions and encouraging debate

427.What is a key benefit of emotional intelligence in students?
a) It helps them manage emotions and build healthy relationships
b) It discourages collaboration
c) It limits creativity
d) It focuses only on academic results
Answer: a) It helps them manage emotions and build healthy relationships

428.What is the main goal of formative assessment?
a) To improve learning by providing timely feedback
b) To replace summative assessments
c) To assign final grades only
d) To discourage student questions
Answer: a) To improve learning by providing timely feedback

429.How can teachers promote self-regulation in students?
a) By teaching them to set goals and manage time effectively
b) By focusing only on group tasks
c) By discouraging independent thought
d) By avoiding personal reflection
Answer: a) By teaching them to set goals and manage time effectively

430.What role does scaffolding play in learning?
a) It offers temporary support to help students achieve independence
b) It replaces hands-on learning
c) It discourages exploration
d) It limits student engagement
Answer: a) It offers temporary support to help students achieve independence

431.How does peer learning improve classroom dynamics?
a) It promotes collaboration and shared responsibility
b) It discourages teamwork
c) It replaces teacher involvement

d) It limits student engagement
Answer: a) It promotes collaboration and shared responsibility

432.What is the purpose of continuous assessment?
a) To track progress and provide feedback throughout the learning process
b) To focus only on end-of-course exams
c) To compare students against each other
d) To discourage classroom interaction
Answer: a) To track progress and provide feedback throughout the learning process

433.How can teachers promote inclusive education?
a) By adapting lessons to meet the needs of all students
b) By focusing only on high achievers
c) By grouping students by ability
d) By avoiding cultural diversity
Answer: a) By adapting lessons to meet the needs of all students

434.What is a key feature of reflective learning?
a) Analyzing experiences to improve future learning
b) Memorizing facts without application
c) Avoiding feedback
d) Focusing only on grades
Answer: a) Analyzing experiences to improve future learning

435.How can teachers encourage creativity in the classroom?
a) By providing open-ended projects and activities
b) By limiting exploration
c) By focusing only on textbook-based tasks
d) By discouraging new ideas
Answer: a) By providing open-ended projects and activities

436.How does goal-setting enhance student performance?
a) It gives students direction and helps track progress
b) It limits creativity
c) It discourages personal reflection
d) It focuses only on outcomes
Answer: a) It gives students direction and helps track progress

437.What is the benefit of scaffolding?
a) It provides the right amount of support to build student independence
b) It replaces student-driven learning
c) It discourages group activities
d) It limits exploration
Answer: a) It provides the right amount of support to build student independence

438.How can teachers support emotional development?
a) By creating a supportive environment where students feel safe expressing emotions
b) By avoiding discussions about feelings
c) By focusing only on academic tasks
d) By discouraging teamwork
Answer: a) By creating a supportive environment where students feel safe expressing emotions

439.What is the main purpose of peer feedback?
a) To help students reflect and improve through peer perspectives
b) To replace teacher evaluations
c) To focus only on grades
d) To limit classroom interaction
Answer: a) To help students reflect and improve through peer perspectives

440.How does continuous assessment benefit students?
a) It ensures consistent feedback and tracks progress
b) It eliminates the need for classroom tasks
c) It discourages group work
d) It focuses only on test scores
Answer: a) It ensures consistent feedback and tracks progress

441.How can teachers promote problem-solving?
a) By encouraging exploration and real-world applications
b) By discouraging teamwork
c) By providing only textbook-based tasks
d) By limiting group activities
Answer: a) By encouraging exploration and real-world applications

442.What role does emotional intelligence play in conflict resolution?
a) It helps students manage emotions and empathize with others
b) It discourages teamwork
c) It focuses only on academic performance
d) It limits student interaction
Answer: a) It helps students manage emotions and empathize with others

443.What is a key benefit of formative assessment?
a) It improves learning through timely feedback and adjustment
b) It eliminates continuous monitoring
c) It discourages participation
d) It replaces classroom discussions
Answer: a) It improves learning through timely feedback and adjustment

444.How can teachers promote intrinsic motivation?
a) By creating meaningful tasks connected to students' interests
b) By relying only on rewards
c) By discouraging exploration
d) By limiting autonomy
Answer: a) By creating meaningful tasks connected to students' interests

445.What is the goal of project-based learning?
a) To engage students in solving real-world challenges
b) To focus only on individual tasks
c) To avoid collaborative efforts
d) To limit critical thinking
Answer: a) To engage students in solving real-world challenges

446.How can teachers create an inclusive environment?
a) By fostering respect and valuing diversity among students
b) By grouping students by ability
c) By focusing only on academic results
d) By discouraging teamwork
Answer: a) By fostering respect and valuing diversity among students

447.How does reflection benefit students?
a) It allows them to analyze their experiences and improve performance
b) It discourages independent thought
c) It focuses only on outcomes
d) It limits creativity
Answer: a) It allows them to analyze their experiences and improve performance

448.How does peer learning enhance understanding?
a) It promotes active participation and knowledge sharing
b) It eliminates the need for feedback
c) It discourages group discussions
d) It focuses only on competition
Answer: a) It promotes active participation and knowledge sharing

449.What is the role of motivation in academic success?
a) It encourages students to persist and engage in learning tasks
b) It discourages personal reflection
c) It focuses only on final results
d) It eliminates feedback
Answer: a) It encourages students to persist and engage in learning tasks

450.How can teachers encourage independent thinking?
a) By promoting inquiry and exploration
b) By avoiding challenging topics
c) By focusing only on memorization
d) By discouraging questions
Answer: a) By promoting inquiry and exploration

451.What is a benefit of project-based learning?
a) It promotes teamwork and critical thinking
b) It discourages creativity
c) It focuses only on theoretical concepts
d) It limits collaboration
Answer: a) It promotes teamwork and critical thinking

452.How can teachers support students from diverse backgrounds?
a) By incorporating cultural relevance into lessons
b) By ignoring diversity
c) By treating all students the same way
d) By avoiding group work
Answer: a) By incorporating cultural relevance into lessons

453.How does emotional intelligence enhance learning?
a) It improves relationships and emotional management
b) It discourages teamwork
c) It focuses only on grades
d) It limits student interaction
Answer: a) It improves relationships and emotional management

454.How can teachers use scaffolding effectively?
a) By gradually reducing support as students gain confidence
b) By avoiding student questions
c) By focusing only on easy tasks
d) By eliminating group work
Answer: a) By gradually reducing support as students gain confidence

455.How can teachers promote creativity in students?
a) By providing opportunities for open-ended exploration
b) By focusing only on textbook learning
c) By discouraging experimentation
d) By limiting student ideas
Answer: a) By providing opportunities for open-ended exploration

456.How does self-assessment benefit students?
a) It encourages reflection and responsibility for learning
b) It eliminates the need for feedback
c) It focuses only on final outcomes
d) It discourages independent thought
Answer: a) It encourages reflection and responsibility for learning

457.What is the goal of continuous and comprehensive evaluation (CCE)?
a) To monitor and improve both academic and non-academic areas
b) To eliminate classroom activities
c) To focus only on exam results
d) To discourage non-academic learning
Answer: a) To monitor and improve both academic and non-academic areas

458.How does peer learning benefit students?
a) It fosters teamwork and deeper understanding through collaboration
b) It discourages social interaction
c) It limits learning to individual activities
d) It replaces teacher instruction
Answer: a) It fosters teamwork and deeper understanding through collaboration

459.How can teachers foster motivation?
a) By designing meaningful and engaging learning experiences
b) By focusing only on outcomes
c) By discouraging creativity
d) By limiting student autonomy
Answer: a) By designing meaningful and engaging learning experiences

460.How does emotional intelligence influence classroom behavior?
a) It helps students manage emotions and build positive relationships
b) It eliminates social interaction
c) It focuses only on individual tasks
d) It discourages teamwork
Answer: a) It helps students manage emotions and build positive relationships

461.What is a benefit of project-based learning?
a) It promotes hands-on learning and critical thinking
b) It focuses only on memorization
c) It discourages collaboration
d) It limits student engagement
Answer: a) It promotes hands-on learning and critical thinking

462.How can teachers support students with learning challenges?
a) By providing individualized strategies and support
b) By treating all students identically
c) By avoiding group activities
d) By limiting feedback
Answer: a) By providing individualized strategies and support

463.How can reflection improve learning?
a) It helps students analyze their experiences and identify improvements
b) It focuses only on final results
c) It discourages personal growth
d) It eliminates feedback
Answer: a) It helps students analyze their experiences and identify improvements

464.What is a key characteristic of inquiry-based learning?
a) Encouraging curiosity and exploration
b) Limiting student interaction
c) Memorizing content without understanding
d) Avoiding real-world applications
Answer: a) Encouraging curiosity and exploration

465.How can teachers promote critical thinking?
a) By encouraging students to question assumptions
b) By focusing only on answers
c) By discouraging debate
d) By limiting discussions
Answer: a) By encouraging students to question assumptions

466.What is the role of feedback in learning?
a) It guides students to improve their performance
b) It eliminates the need for reflection
c) It discourages student engagement
d) It focuses only on mistakes
Answer: a) It guides students to improve their performance

467.How can teachers foster collaboration?
a) By assigning group tasks that require teamwork
b) By focusing only on individual work
c) By discouraging interaction
d) By limiting peer feedback
Answer: a) By assigning group tasks that require teamwork

468.How does motivation affect learning?
a) It encourages students to engage and persevere
b) It eliminates the need for effort
c) It discourages student participation
d) It focuses only on grades
Answer: a) It encourages students to engage and persevere

469.What is a key benefit of self-assessment?
a) It helps students take responsibility for their own learning
b) It discourages independent thinking
c) It focuses only on outcomes
d) It eliminates personal reflection
Answer: a) It helps students take responsibility for their own learning

470.How can teachers promote inclusive education?
a) By valuing diversity and accommodating all students
b) By focusing only on high achievers
c) By grouping students by ability
d) By avoiding discussions about inclusion
Answer: a) By valuing diversity and accommodating all students

471.How does scaffolding benefit students?
a) It provides temporary support to build independence
b) It limits critical thinking
c) It discourages exploration
d) It replaces hands-on learning
Answer: a) It provides temporary support to build independence

472.What is a feature of continuous assessment?
a) Providing regular feedback to monitor progress
b) Conducting only final exams
c) Eliminating classroom interaction
d) Focusing solely on competition
Answer: a) Providing regular feedback to monitor progress

473.How can teachers encourage problem-solving skills?
a) By promoting real-world challenges and critical thinking
b) By focusing only on memorization
c) By discouraging teamwork
d) By avoiding complex problems
Answer: a) By promoting real-world challenges and critical thinking

474.What is the role of peer feedback?
a) It promotes reflection and improvement through collaboration
b) It replaces teacher feedback
c) It focuses only on final grades
d) It discourages teamwork
Answer: a) It promotes reflection and improvement through collaboration

475.How does emotional intelligence affect teamwork?
a) It helps students manage emotions and work effectively with others
b) It discourages collaboration
c) It focuses only on individual tasks
d) It limits communication
Answer: a) It helps students manage emotions and work effectively with others

476.How can teachers create a growth mindset?
a) By praising effort and resilience in students
b) By focusing only on outcomes
c) By avoiding difficult tasks
d) By discouraging self-reflection
Answer: a) By praising effort and resilience in students

477.What is the goal of project-based learning?
a) To engage students in solving real-world problems
b) To eliminate teamwork
c) To focus only on individual tasks
d) To discourage exploration
Answer: a) To engage students in solving real-world problems

478.How can reflection enhance learning?
a) By helping students analyze what worked and what didn't
b) By discouraging independent thought
c) By focusing only on grades
d) By limiting creativity
Answer: a) By helping students analyze what worked and what didn't

479.How does peer learning benefit students?
a) It fosters collaboration and shared understanding
b) It eliminates classroom interaction
c) It discourages teamwork
d) It limits engagement
Answer: a) It fosters collaboration and shared understanding

480.How can teachers promote critical thinking?
a) By asking students to explore multiple perspectives
b) By focusing only on correct answers
c) By avoiding complex questions
d) By limiting discussion
Answer: a) By asking students to explore multiple perspectives

481.How does continuous assessment support learning?
a) By providing feedback throughout the course
b) By focusing only on final grades
c) By discouraging participation
d) By eliminating reflection
Answer: a) By providing feedback throughout the course

482.What is the purpose of scaffolding?
a) To help students progress with temporary support
b) To replace independent learning
c) To limit exploration
d) To discourage questions
Answer: a) To help students progress with temporary support

483.How can teachers support diverse learners?
a) By providing differentiated instruction
b) By treating all students identically
c) By ignoring individual needs
d) By discouraging inclusion
Answer: a) By providing differentiated instruction

484.How does goal-setting improve performance?
a) It helps students stay focused and motivated
b) It discourages personal reflection
c) It limits exploration
d) It eliminates feedback
Answer: a) It helps students stay focused and motivated

485.What is a feature of reflective learning?
a) Analyzing experiences to enhance future performance
b) Avoiding critical thinking
c) Focusing only on grades
d) Discouraging self-reflection
Answer: a) Analyzing experiences to enhance future performance

486.How can teachers foster collaboration?
a) By assigning group tasks that require teamwork
b) By focusing only on individual tasks
c) By discouraging interaction
d) By eliminating group projects
Answer: a) By assigning group tasks that require teamwork

487.How does emotional intelligence benefit students?
a) It helps them manage emotions and empathize with others
b) It discourages teamwork
c) It limits communication
d) It focuses only on grades
Answer: a) It helps them manage emotions and empathize with others

488.What is the goal of inclusive education?
a) To provide equitable learning opportunities for all students
b) To separate students based on ability
c) To focus only on academic performance
d) To discourage diversity
Answer: a) To provide equitable learning opportunities for all students

489.How can teachers promote motivation?
a) By creating meaningful and engaging tasks
b) By limiting feedback
c) By avoiding exploration
d) By discouraging autonomy
Answer: a) By creating meaningful and engaging tasks

490.What is the benefit of peer learning?
a) It encourages students to learn from each other
b) It eliminates teamwork
c) It discourages interaction
d) It limits exploration
Answer: a) It encourages students to learn from each other

491.How does feedback improve learning?
a) It guides students in refining their understanding and skills
b) It focuses only on errors without solutions
c) It discourages student reflection
d) It eliminates the need for assessments
Answer: a) It guides students in refining their understanding and skills

492.How can teachers support students with learning difficulties?
a) By offering personalized strategies and consistent feedback
b) By avoiding individual attention
c) By assigning identical tasks to all students
d) By limiting participation in group work
Answer: a) By offering personalized strategies and consistent feedback

493.What role does motivation play in independent learning?
a) It encourages students to take initiative and stay engaged
b) It eliminates the need for exploration
c) It discourages self-assessment
d) It focuses only on external rewards
Answer: a) It encourages students to take initiative and stay engaged

494.How can teachers foster teamwork in the classroom?
a) By designing group activities that require collaboration
b) By focusing only on individual tasks
c) By discouraging peer interaction
d) By assigning competitive assessments exclusively
Answer: a) By designing group activities that require collaboration

495.What is a key aspect of project-based learning?
a) Solving real-world problems through practical applications
b) Memorizing facts without discussion
c) Avoiding teamwork
d) Focusing only on theoretical knowledge
Answer: a) Solving real-world problems through practical applications

496.How does reflection help students improve?
a) It allows them to analyze their learning and make adjustments
b) It focuses only on final grades
c) It discourages critical thinking
d) It limits creative exploration
Answer: a) It allows them to analyze their learning and make adjustments

497.What is the purpose of formative assessment?
a) To provide ongoing feedback for continuous improvement
b) To assign final grades only
c) To focus exclusively on end-of-term exams
d) To replace collaborative learning activities
Answer: a) To provide ongoing feedback for continuous improvement

498.How can teachers promote inclusive learning?
a) By accommodating individual differences and fostering diversity
b) By focusing only on high achievers
c) By discouraging collaboration among students
d) By treating all students identically without adjustment
Answer: a) By accommodating individual differences and fostering diversity

499.What is the benefit of self-assessment?
a) It helps students take ownership of their learning and progress
b) It eliminates the need for reflection
c) It focuses only on external rewards
d) It discourages independent thinking
Answer: a) It helps students take ownership of their learning and progress

500.How does peer learning enhance classroom engagement?
a) It encourages active participation and shared learning experiences
b) It discourages teamwork and collaboration
c) It focuses only on competition among students
d) It limits student involvement
Answer: a) It encourages active participation and shared learning experiences